FLAWED AND (STILL) WORTHY

FLAWED AND (STILL) WORTHY

Owning Your Journey and Embracing Your Flaws

ALLIE BRAZAS

LIONCREST

PUBLISHING

FLAWED AND (STILL) WORTHY

Owning Your Journey and Embracing Your Flaws

ISBN   978-1-5445-0609-8 *Hardcover*

978-1-5445-0607-4 *Paperback*

978-1-5445-0608-1 *Ebook*

978-1-5445-0650-0 *Audiobook*

Addisen Jade,

This book was written for you. I hope the words and stories found within the depths of these pages serve as gentle reminders never to allow the pain of what's behind you keep you from experiencing the beauty that's ahead of you.

Love you to the moon,

Mom

CONTENTS

INTRODUCTION

ON COMPETITION

When I was seven, my family took a week-long summer vacation to California. We periodically ventured out to popular tourist attractions and dinner joints, but agreed to spend most of our time by the ocean. As I remember it, every day the sun shone, the water was warm, and our faces fried. My brother Luke loved diving headfirst into the waves over and over again, boogie board in hand, wearing solid blue swim trunks and an infectious smile, while I preferred to park it on the sand. Sandwiched safely between my parents' beach chairs, I spent whole afternoons molding the sparkly sand and daydreaming about the kind of fairytale life I would someday have for myself.

My sand art would change, but the story always stayed

the same. A circular mound was my castle. My white sand rake made the perfect picket fence. The dirty blue sand bucket was my husband. I was the red sand scoop. Together we stood watch over a brood of multicolored seashell children. When everything was hard-packed and placed just so, I'd pronounce my empire complete. My version of the future looked so quintessential and grand laid out in the sand. The idea that things could turn out any other way never even crossed my radar.

But just like the old proverb says: hindsight is 20/20.

By ten, I'd learned a thing or two about fairytales. They are not, for example, immune to competition. I may still have been in the daydreaming stage, but comparisons were starting to emerge—good, better, best—as I first sized myself up next to those closest to me (my parents, my brother), followed by those who had what I wanted (my peers). It would spur me to do, be, and strive for more, until finally there'd be just one opponent left to beat: the one staring back at me in the mirror.

When you look at yourself in the mirror, what do you see? Someone standing tall and confident, proud of all the shit she's been through and overcome? Or does your head hang low, your shoulders stooped beneath the shame of where you've been and discouragement at how far you still have to go?

The answer to that question will determine if you should keep reading.

MY OWN WORST CRITIC

When I begrudgingly looked in the mirror—at ten, at twelve, at eighteen, at twenty-five—I consistently found an exceptionally flawed reflection staring back at me. Exhaustion from the horrific trauma I had endured and the pain I had survived left scars that made my sand-molded future seem far out of reach. The sandcastle family and all the dreams that went with it began slowly drifting away with the tide. Haunted by the remnants of my past, I no longer felt worthy of a future so dreamy, so perfect.

I was always my own worst critic, constantly competing against myself. I habitually held myself to impossible standards, and when I tried but failed to meet them, I never praised my efforts. There were no, "Atta-boys." No, "You'll do better next time." I didn't acknowledge my hard work in the mirror because all I saw was a defective little girl, slumped over and disgraced.

At seven, I didn't think my fairytale future was a huge stretch. A spouse, a house, some kids—I mean, let's be real: most humans desire those things. But after I'd done everything in the wrong order (pregnant before marriage;

a missed deployment that subsequently tarnished my career), it made a sick kind of sense that my husband would perish and my entire world would be threatened by a man who used and abused his high-ranking power. My life no longer looked like my family's lives, or my friends' lives, or even the lives of the strangers who lived next door. My life looked discombobulated and completely out of control, and it was all I could do to try and keep up with the Joneses.

That's what we as women do to ourselves: exacerbate life's already hard times by comparing ourselves to others, placing ourselves in a competition that neither participant wants to be in. I'm not saying it's entirely our fault—the societal standards we're held to definitely play a role—but ladies, WE are in control of how we respond to those expectations. Women are expected to smile, be polite, brush our hair, not get fat, not get too thin, not be too boisterous, not be too shy, and the list goes on and on. If you don't fit the perfect mold, you're "unworthy" in the eyes of others. You know what I say? FUCK THAT! Absolutely NONE of that matters unless you give in to those ridiculously impossible standards—and most damning of all, see yourself as unworthy, like I once did.

Whatever your demon, it's likely a perceived lack: of prettiness, money, education, love, fairness, or a million other ghosts. The pain from all you are "lacking" consumes you and before you know it, you're the shame-faced reflection staring back at you, wondering when shit will begin to turn around for you. Well, ladies: that moment is now. NOW is when we turn all that you're "lacking" into strengths you didn't know you had.

THE BAR

Much like the tide, our annual California vacations came and went, and so did time. Before I knew it, I'd made it to freshman year of high school and I was desperate to keep up with my senior brother's legacy of being great at, well, pretty much everything. A diehard cheerleader since I could properly carry a pom-pom, I knew I needed to mix things up, so I signed up for the track and field team—pole vault, specifically. Although I'd never attempted a jump that wasn't associated with cheer, I couldn't pass up the opportunity to prove to myself that not only was I an athlete, but I was the kind whose name lives on in school record books.

The first time I saw that thirty-two-inch-thick mat, that excessively long pole, and that ridiculously high bar, I felt excited. Finally, a worthy challenge! I wasn't at all sure I could do it, but if I could, my family would surely discuss it around the dinner table that night! After the coach's brief overview, we lined up, and one by one took a running start toward our destinies. Who among us would leave the ground, launching herself gracefully over the bar, clearing it cleanly? Could it be me? As my turn inched ever closer, I pepped myself up. Perfection, Al. Nothing less.

My palms were clammy, my legs shaky, and beads of nervous sweat peppered my brow when the coach gave me the go-ahead. I ran, pole in hand, focused and strong. Planting the pole firmly in its socket, I gripped it tightly and arched my body skyward. Interminable seconds later, I landed on the soft mat, elated at not having touched the bar once. I didn't immediately realize that wasn't because I'd cleared it—but because I'd flung myself rather ungracefully under it. Standing up, I walked off the mat grinning ear to ear. Then I turned around and saw my teammates laughing (not necessarily at me, but with me). That's when I realized my failure to launch. While I gamely chuckled along, a heat wave of anger, coupled with a heaping spoonful of embarrassment, grew just beneath my overly loud, insecurity-masking belly laugh.

Even then, I was skilled at converting embarrassment to anger, because anger was useful. It fueled me. Anger made me get up and try again. Anger drove me to refine my technique, to attack the bar with single-minded purpose, to elevate it to a symbol of perfection. There on a track in Tempe, Arizona, I arbitrarily created my very own bunch of impossible standards—the "bar" that I set for myself—the bar that I never did clear. It would haunt me for years to come, forever representing every goal I would name and inevitably not meet.

The thing about competing against yourself is, you never can win. At the moment a winner gets declared, so does, by implication, a loser.

SWIMMING IN ROUGH SEAS

Eventually I'd learn to channel my anger at myself and my "faults" in more constructive ways. By then, I'd be a sailor, a mother, a widow, and a wife. I'd be ripped from the security of the sandy shore and thrown into the volatile depths, where things get scary and standing on your own two feet is impossible. I'd realize that life itself is bigger than my desire to control it.

Lost at sea, as I was for most of my twenties, I nevertheless continued fighting. Caught in a riptide that threatened to drown me, I kept treading water in pursuit of the "bar." The only way to reach it, I thought, was to keep it in my sights; and the only way to do that was to make damn sure I kept my head above water.

It's terribly hard to tread in a storm. You take in all kinds of water, all kinds of salt to the wounds, and it burns and you choke and you flail. You grow resentful. You never asked for a life like this! If you chase something long enough, however, one of three things happens: you achieve whatever it is you're after; exhaustion creeps in and you quit; or as in my case, you eventually change course entirely.

Part of growing up is forsaking the mentality that lifeboats exist. LADIES, no one's coming to save you! You can save yourself on your own. I thought that if I joined the military and made rank, or had a baby, or any number of markers of success, that I would finally make it. That I would be saved from oblivion. What I needed saving from, though, was my own victimhood: the idea that I was a victim of circumstance. Forget lifeboats; I was the only one who could have pulled myself out of that water. No wonder an endless list of achievements couldn't spare me. Rather, it was the lessons that hardship taught me along the way—or the lessons that working toward a dream drew out of me. Everything I needed was already inside me. I just couldn't hear myself over the waves.

The good news is that you already have everything you need, too, whether you're aware of it or not. Right now, all you see are flaws. Which makes sense—the panic we feel as we drown isn't rational. So calm down, trust the water to support you, and rein in your survival instincts. As you do this, you may find yourself drifting just a tiny bit further from shore. That's okay! Getting back to a place where your feet can touch the bottom is the goal, but there are many ways to do so.

My route was never direct. If anything, it was a water flume, with steep falls and hairpin turns. I rarely saw what was coming next. Had I succumbed to anger, to victimhood, to self-pity, I may have literally given in to the waves before I got the chance to learn what the water had come to teach me. Yes, we are all single drops in a vast and violent ocean, but in 2010, eleven other women and I would come together to make a splash of our own, championing the rights of women and seeing justice served. My beautiful, sweet daughter would add her own drop to the water. And somehow, amazingly, adrift amongst all the other drops, I'd find a partner meant just for me. And we'd float on together.

FLAWED AND (STILL) WORTHY

This book was born from a blog I began keeping in 2013, just after the death of my husband Sean. The blog was a way to make sense of my time in the military, process my feelings, share stories with family and friends, and overall "control" the narrative that was being spun about me, like a suffocating cocoon, during my time of greatest grief. I was doing everything within my power to handle this tragedy the "right" way. Through blogging, I could keep up "perfect widow" appearances while withholding all the pieces that fell short of that objective.

Since then I've learned a better way that isn't all about control and perfection.

Flawed and (Still) Worthy is not that blog. It doesn't sugarcoat anything, spin anything, or hold back on anything at all. There are stories in here that only my family and my closest friends—my Circle of Trust—knew about, until now. As you'll learn in chapter 10, I've come to value transparency as one of the cornerstones of my life.

Along with acceptance, perseverance, resiliency, and more, each chapter explores a central theme or lesson that I've learned from the various chapters of my life. Collectively, they helped me get back to shore and stop the perpetual cycle of dreaming, striving, and beating myself up, competing against my own shadow side. All of these are healthy alternatives to perfectionism, and unlike the bar, can actually help you achieve your fairytale, even—and especially—when the odds seem stacked against you.

If you're out there treading water, hold on. I'm coming for you.

ON PERFECTION

If you're lucky, you get one best friend in life who stays by your side no matter what. I met Bridget in kindergarten, and to this day she's still my number one: the cornerstone of my inner circle, what I call my Circle of Trust. Bridget and I have been through just about everything together, including the specific trials of middle school in millennial America.

In 2000, I was eleven years old and immersed in the Christina Aguilera/Britney Spears craze. These two pop stars defined everything "cool," from clothing (crop tops and hiphugger jeans) to hairstyles (the crimp, anyone?), and the message was clear: You should want to look like me. In addition to fashion trends, they ushered in the long, lean frame, completely at odds with the developing body of a middle schooler. While Kim Kardashian curves may be all the rage these days, when I compared myself to Britney or Christina, I saw a girl who was just plain fat. The clothes they told me to wear weren't meant for a body like mine. I bulged in all the wrong places. I was someone who could never fit in.

Luckily, Bridget was right there with me. Neither of us had been blessed with a double-zero waist or tiny stick legs. We had thighs that touched, wider hips, arms just beginning to show their baby muscles. To adults, we were "athletically built" and perfectly normal for our pre-pubescent selves, but as far as we could tell, we were a far cry from anything "normal." We wanted to be perfect, period—as measured by society's impossible standards.

Starting in sixth grade, we took to running every morning on the canal behind my house. One complete lap around the canal was two miles. Every day, before the sun had fully risen in the sky, we'd run the first mile together, then walk the second as we talked and caught up. From there, we'd go back to my house, grab two mocha-flavored Slim Fasts, and walk the half-mile to school.

While we were running, I would fantasize about having the "perfect" body, playing out in my head how every-thing in my life would change for the better once I was skinny. I wouldn't have to worry about my shorts rubbing anymore, or how I looked in the most popular tops. Kids would stop teasing me because I finally conformed to their standards. In retrospect, I can see that the image we were striving for was that of a perpetual eight-year-old's body, no budding womanliness to it at all.

The thing is, our plan worked. By getting two and a half miles in before anyone else had even gotten up to brush their teeth, I forced my body into compliance and it obeyed. I never stopped to wonder why I cared so much, or question why I wanted to be like everyone else. If I had, I might have realized something about my motivations. For me, it wasn't enough to merely fit the perfect mold in my own eyes; I needed other people to validate my efforts, for the popular kids to comment on my weight loss or invite me to their birthday parties. It didn't matter how I felt physically, so long as the world around me recognized my physical self as normal. Then, and only then, I believed, could I be accepted—when my peers said, "Cute Hollister shirt!" because I finally fit into one.

This preoccupation morphed into a lifelong chase after perfection that would manifest in all the ways that mattered: at school, at home, and in my personal life. Almost everything I did from this point onward, I did for acceptance, I did for self-worth.

SUCCESS AT ANY COST

The only daughter of an ambitious, hardworking mother and a devoted Lutheran father, I often joke that my whole life would have been easier if I'd only been born a boy. I had an older brother, Luke, who seemed to sail through life, setting weightlifting records as he flexed his six-pack and winning positive attention effortlessly. I'm not saying he didn't have his fair share of struggles, but man, he sure made them all look so conquerable. My parents were proud of him—rightfully so—and their relationship seemed equally easy.

I, on the other hand, was melodramatic, hormonal, and average at pretty much everything. I worked tirelessly at cheer, at academics, at my athleticism, but I always seemed to wind up in the middle of the pack. Never ahead, never exceptional, always just enough.

The older I got, the more I threw myself into every pursuit under the sun, and with the same fervor. I ran track and cross-country through freshman year of high school, then continued on with competitive cheer, a sport I'd started at six years old. Freshman year I also ran for student council. I had this dream of becoming class president, because it meant winning more votes than any other candidate. I turned the high beams on with my energy and enthusiasm, and spent my days passing out flyers that read "Put Your Tally on Allie" with candy attached.

Just like it had with the running, my hard work paid off. I remember when they made the announcement. Oh my gosh, I thought, this is so awesome! But my excitement was quickly tempered by a persistent shadow thought: Exemplary, Al—nothing short of perfection. Average just won't do this time around.

Even though I quit track after that year, the bar from my pole-vaulting days haunted me. It symbolized something that I'd attempted and failed at, which became one and the same with my self-defeating perfectionism. Everything I achieved should have been like clearing the bar: a clean jump! Instead, each achievement moved the bar a little higher, taunting me with its insistence that while I might have done it one time, I couldn't do it again.

THE PERCEPTION OF CONTROL

Perfectionism has its roots in control: sometimes over others, but more often over the self—and especially, in my case, the body. While I was never diagnosed with an eating disorder, my sixth-grade Slim Fast habit metamorphosed to a "number system," wherein beginning in high school I never let myself eat more than three things a day. As three things didn't tick off the fingers of a whole hand, it was a manageable, forgivable, amount of food. Even on splurge days I wouldn't eat more than five things, because that would bump me onto a second hand, or what I believed was an unacceptable amount of food to consume. It didn't make any sense, but it gave me the perception of control.

I lived by that "system" for years. While I can't say that it made me happy, exactly, it gave me the kind of body I could tolerate in a cheer uniform—and that did make me happy.*

Cheer—and thereby, dieting—also met a very real social need. Starting sophomore year, I noticed my peers were changing. They were growing up, acting out, throwing parties, and drinking. I felt left out since I wasn't often invited to those parties and I didn't drink anyway. Breaking the law never did jibe with my whole pursuit of control and perfection. Everyone showed up Monday morning with wild stories and inside jokes that I didn't know. The pressure to still fit in in some way spurred on my over-commitment to school activities and my ill-informed approach to nutrition.

By junior year, I'd (predictably) burnt myself out. I didn't want to run anymore, not for track or student council.

---

* Only now that I have a daughter do I understand just how warped this form of "happiness" is. All I wanted was to *not be fat* because "fat"' wasn't "perfect" in the eyes of my peers. Today "fat" is the f-word in my house, by which I mean that my daughter knows never to say it. I'd rather she said "fuck" than "fat," because I don't want her to grow up with the idea that a) being fat is the end of the world (it's not) or b) "fat" is a word you can use cavalierly (it's not; it damages people for life).

I'd tried out for and made the varsity cheer squad, but the mere thought of keeping up the image necessary for cheerleading exhausted me. I wanted to be able to focus on academics and nothing else. I thought if academics were the only thing I had to worry about, my grades would be exceptional. I talked my parents into letting me enroll at the accelerated school next to my high school. A very controlled and focused environment, it was good for me. I flourished there. I made high grades and earned enough credits to graduate in March of 2006, a school year ahead of my classmates at Marcos de Niza High.

Rather than go back to Big Surf Waterpark, where I'd worked the past four summers, I looked around for an interesting entry-level career. At the waterpark, I'd variously been a lifeguard, a supervisor, and a "Red One" (the aquatic assistant manager who trains the lifeguards). I loved helping people; the adrenaline of responding to a medical emergency gave me a high that couldn't be matched. For that reason, medicine appealed to me. I briefly considered nursing, but every school in the state had a three-year waitlist. Becoming a medical assistant, on the other hand, required just a nine-month certificate program. I'd be licensed to work for a doctor or a hospital by the time my high school friends were graduating. Now that was taking control of my (incredibly bright) future!

In January 2007, a semester before my class would join

the workforce, I got a job at a private clinic in Tempe. The work came easy to me, and so did the acceptance I'd been seeking for years. Patients were routinely shocked by my age when I walked into the exam room. "My God, you're so young to be working here!" they'd exclaim, or "Aren't you just the prettiest thing?" My doctor encouraged me, too. "I can't believe how fast you've caught on," he would say. "Keep up the hard work." Inside, I allowed myself a tiny celebration. You're ahead, Allie. Not only have you met the bar, you've cleared it with room to spare.

My cup now overflowing with validation, I cautiously let my guard down. I stopped watching for the waves.

At seventeen, I'd get swept out with the riptide altogether.

THAT DAY

Shortly after beginning my medical career, I joined a gym in Tempe. Without sports to keep me in shape, I planned to use the gym's cardio equipment. A sales guy approached me almost as soon as I walked through the door. "What's up?" he asked. "I'm John. How can I help you today?"

I listened to John ramble about the benefits of membership and answered the same million questions he probably asked everyone who stopped in. Naive, I didn't realize I was being sold. I thought, Oh, he's nice and seems really interested in helping me meet my goals! Today I roll my eyes at such innocence, but it's why, when he asked what time I'd be coming to work out next, I answered honestly and without a second thought. "Tomorrow morning."

"Awesome. Do you know how to use all the machines?"

"Not really."

"Well, if you want, I could train you."

I considered his jacked arms. "That would be great. How much does it cost?"

"For you, nothing. I'll be working out then anyway, so it's no big deal. We can train together."

WOW! WOW! AND WOW! To a sixteen-year-old working a minimum-wage job, anything FREE was music to my young, virgin ears.

We trained together every day. John would tell me what to do that day—how many jumping jacks, how many miles, how many pounds on the bar—and I'd perform, perfectly. In between sets, he shared snippets of his personal life. He had a girlfriend and three kids. He'd recently been released from prison and was living at a halfway house.

Instead of scaring me, his story inspired me. I saw a twenty-eight-year-old man doing everything right to get his life back on track. He was friendly and funny and his coworkers loved him. Good for him, I thought. Everybody makes mistakes.

Even Allie.

One day, John took me to the back storage closet. We'd met there a couple times before when he wanted to tell me a private story. The closet was empty except for some boxes and a bench where we'd sit and chat, and from which I would console him. On this day, things were different. "Allie Cat," he said, which was the nickname he always called me by. "I think I really like you, Allie Cat."

"Aw, I like you, too," I said.

"No...I really like you."

"Haha, sick joke, you have a girlfriend, Grandpa." I was trying to let him down easy.

"None of that matters when I'm with you."

Was I flattered? Yes. Was I also worried about the people who stood to be hurt by this conversation? (I did not include myself in that category.) Double yes.

"That's really sweet, John, but I can't do this with you."

"I think I like you so much I'm going to fuck you," John said.

Um, what?

Before I could react, John had locked the closet door, pulled my spandex down, shoved me face first into the wall, and shoved himself inside of me. Not only did he rape me, but it was not the correct hole. And THAT, ladies and gentlemen, is how I lost my virginity.

The most horribly ironic part of this whole story is that prior to his assault, I was the thinnest I had ever been. My hip bones stuck out further than my stomach. I was getting all the compliments. Between my physique and my early career accomplishments, I really thought I had it all. I never again came as close as I was then to clearing the bar.

After that day, I found my formerly perfect body disgusting. I hated myself. I went from wearing cute tank tops and shorts to the gym to full-on sweats and long sleeves. Although I switched locations, I couldn't stop looking over my shoulder for John's shadow. When I told an adult close to me, she chose not to believe me. So I dealt with my trauma the way I always had and would continue to do for most of my young adult life: Alone. Raw. Silenced.

From that point on, no matter how hard I tried, I knew I could never reach perfection. I was dirty, unlovable, unworthy, and completely imperfect. How do you "jog off," or "sweat out," or "restrict your food intake of" rape? You don't. I hadn't asked to be assaulted, but still it had happened, and in the process I had tarnished any shot I ever had of being exemplary or worthy or perfect or loved. Gone was the girl who'd built sandcastles blissfully in the sun. She'd been pulled out to sea by an undertow she hadn't recognized, and no one was coming to save her.

ON IMPERFECTION

Driving through the hustle and bustle of rush-hour traffic on my way home from another twelve-hour shift, I found myself contemplating my next move. Despite the beauty of the brilliant sun setting before me, I felt stagnant. I had been a medical assistant for two years. My friends from high school had finally graduated and begun their journeys at major universities across the nation. Although I'd worked hard to get the job I now had, for the first time, it seemed rather middle-of-the-road—paling in comparison to the opportunities suddenly available to everyone else. My achievement wasn't "new and shiny" anymore. I need something better, I thought. More challenging. More fulfilling.

While waiting for the traffic light to turn green, I noticed a military recruiting station across the street. Posters in the windows advertised for the Coast Guard, Navy, Army, and Marines. They showed strong, fit individuals engaged in bettering themselves and their country. I recalled the statistic that approximately one percent of Americans serve in the military. My grandfather and a cousin had been among their numbers. Oh my God, I realized, that's it. What could possibly more challenging and fulfilling than the United States military?

I'd always loved my country, and like the majority of America, had been emotionally moved by the tragedy of 9/11. Until this moment, enlisting had never crossed my mind—but once it did, I felt called to act immediately. When the light changed, I drove through it, turned left, and pulled into the first empty parking spot. Directly ahead of me was the recruiting office for the Navy. I took it as a sign and walked through their doors. Two young guys in their late twenties greeted me. "How can we help you today?" they asked, wearing identical shit-eating grins.

"Well, I would like to join the Navy," I announced.

"Cool. Why the Navy?"

"I was a lifeguard for four years, I'm a great swimmer, and I love boats!"

The sailors glanced at each other and smirked. "You've come to the right place, then."

Nailed it! I thought to myself as I smirked back.

One guy took me through a medical history form and a general questionnaire, most of which concerned my prior drug usage (I'd never tried a drug in my life; double nailed it), before setting me up to take the Armed Services Vocational Aptitude Battery (ASVAB). The test determines: a) if you're intelligent enough to join the service; and b) what job to place you in. I passed every part with flying colors, thinking all the while, Man, this is a lot easier than I thought it'd be. Two hours later, I left with a signed contract in hand and a grin on my face. Crushed it! Not fully aware of what I'd just committed to, I didn't feel the slightest bit of trepidation. Rather, I couldn't wait to get home and tell everyone my news.

As the traffic had pretty well cleared out, I pushed the speed limit all the way back home. Bursting with pride, I strode into my parents' house wearing the world's biggest smile. "Eh-hem. Excuse the interruption, people, but you're now looking at the newest United States Navy recruit," I boasted.

"What?" my mom asked, setting her fork still loaded with food back down on her plate. Both she and my dad looked super confused.

"Guys, I joined the military after work today!"

"Wow," Dad finally said, the first to break the silence. Then, more enthusiastically: "Wow! That's great, Al!"

I joined them at the table and filled them in. No, the military had never been a secret dream of mine. No, I hadn't known I'd wanted to enlist until I'd seen the station. Yes, the sailors had been friendly and nice. ("Yeah, of course they were," my dad chimed in.) No, I hadn't really thought it through, but yes, I felt good about my decision.

That's how I ended up at boot camp in January of 2009.

MISSION ACCEPTED

For any natural-born perfectionist, boot camp is basically heaven. While it's physically and mentally demanding, I've never felt more faultless than I did while training to be a sailor. You're literally told when to wake up, when to go to bed, what to wear, and how to iron your clothes. You're told when to work out and how to work out. You're also told when and where to pee. Some weeks, I went entire days without making a single decision for myself. I found boot camp easy to nail when my instructions were so explicit, versus the days of trying to navigate life successfully when success had taken so many different forms.

I not only excelled at boot camp, I enjoyed it. My body took the constant punishment like a champ, and my mind was already used to stricture and structure (to be fair, I'd imposed these on myself before). I also reveled in the notion that, at just nineteen, I'd moved to Illinois and started a life of my own. How many young people could say that? Not too many. Part of the allure, of course, was the distance boot camp put between me and my rapist, John. More than 1,700 miles and a world of experience separated me from him now. I didn't have time to think or dwell; I merely executed, and in the process, allowed myself to forget.

Boot camp lasted for eight weeks. At graduation, my whole family showed up in support. They beamed with pride as they demanded pictures, set up a celebratory dinner, and showered me with gifts. Playfully, they admitted that they'd taken bets on whether or not I would make it through, which fueled my drive to make my new career a success.

JUST A BLONDE-HAIRED VALLEY GIRL

After boot camp, I wound up in Bremerton, Washington, at Naval Base Kitsap. There I was attached to a submarine tender called the USS Emory S. Land, a dated ship that services submarines and provides food, fuel, spare parts, and repairs as needed. I was further designated part of the small boat division. The USS Emory carried several smaller, detachable boats used for emergencies and for other various reasons. The small boat div maintained these boats and ensured they could be deployed at a moment's notice.

Given my love of boats and water, I was really excited to be assigned to this ship. I couldn't wait to be deployed. Who knew what adventures awaited us at sea? The disappointment hit especially hard, therefore, when I showed up to find the USS Emory dry-docked. It was propped up on stilts in the harbor, all the water drained away so that repairs could be made to the hull of the ship. We wouldn't be deploying any time soon. In fact, the scene at Bremerton was so relaxed that on the day I reported for duty, my chief (who in civilian life is like your manager or direct supervisor) told me to come in civilian clothes. "It's the weekend and no one's here, so there's no need to show up in uniform," he said. Great! I thought. First day on the job and it's Casual Friday!

Let's just say I had a lot of growing up to do—and a lot of growing into the Navy.

I reported to my chief wearing wedges, white Bermuda shorts, and a pink spaghetti-strap top with a white blazer over it, toting a rolling pink zebra suitcase behind me. If you're picturing Elle Woods in Legally Blonde, that would be accurate. Needless to say, it didn't go over well.

I remember walking across the brow—the platform that gets you from the dock to the ship—and seeing my chief's face, which said it all. "What in the actual FUCK are you wearing?" he shouted. Word travels fast on a ship. From that day forward, neither he nor anyone else in my division took me seriously. They'd always comment on my girly accent and insist that I MUST have missed the bus from cheer camp and wound up at bootcamp. My peers were nice enough to me, always taking time to explain what tool was used for what and which screw went where, but at the same time, they made sure I knew my lack of knowledge was horseshit. I was left out a lot, and often not trusted with the simplest tasks. That was difficult for this hard-working medical assistant who was used to her doctor's and patients' respect.

In hindsight, I wouldn't have taken myself seriously, either. I was supposed to be working on small boats, yet I'd never picked up a wrench in my life. Boot camp may prepare you for war, but it doesn't teach you how to tighten a lug-nut. Determined as ever to prove them all wrong, I studied up, sought help when I needed it, and generally set about becoming a better sailor. Whenever feelings of helplessness, defeat, or all-around outsiderness (none of which were new feelings to me) threatened to overwhelm me, I pushed through them in pursuit of becoming an asset to the team.

As if to make me accept, once and for all, my utter imperfection, however, life would throw me another curveball: my most spectacular failing yet.

SIX STICKS, SIX POSITIVES

His name was Keith, and boy did he have an ability to crack me up! Humor has always been one of the top qualities I look for in men, so when Keith became my personal comedian, I fell hard for him. One of my superiors introduced us my first night standing watch (even in dry dock, we roved the deck armed, guarding the ship 24/7). "Haz," he said—a nickname born from my maiden name of Hasenwinkel—"this is Keith. Keith, Haz."

Keith walked the deck with me the rest of the night, telling jokes that had me bent over in pain from hysterically laughing. He was a year older than me (twenty) and, I would learn, ambitious. We started hanging out regularly after that, which evolved into dating in late 2009. Navy instruction stipulated that you could date, but not marry, sailors in your same command, so we didn't have to hide our relationship or worry about breaking any rules.

One cold and crisp January day, my crew mates and I were

scraping the hulls of our ship's small boats. I was working on the Captain's rig, his personal small boat, and chipping away at the nasty grime and algae that boats accumulate over time. It smelled bad—like dead fish and seaweed—but having been exposed to some of the raunchiest smells known to man in the medical field, odors never bothered me. On this day, though, the stench from the hull sent me hurling overboard.

"Holy shit, Haz! Are you sick or are you pregnant?" one of my shipmates shouted.

"Sick, for sure!" I yelled back—but inside, I knew it was the latter.

After work, I called my barracks roommate, Danielle, and explained what had happened. She sensed the urgency in my voice and agreed to meet me at the Navy Exchange right down the street from our ship. I bought six different pregnancy tests and beelined for the Exchange bathroom. Danielle stood outside the stall while I peed on each and every one of the six sticks. By the end of the ordeal, we were both standing at the bathroom sink staring at six positives.

All that was running through my mind, once the shock wore off, was: Oh my God. The one thing you're never supposed to do as a female in the military is get pregnant while assigned to a ship. Literally, it's the most important unwritten but outwardly observed rule in the Navy, and I had just broken it. I didn't have to wait for my leaders and peers to punish me; I began punishing my psyche as soon as I found out. I thought about all the people I was going to let down: my crew (we were finally about to be deployed), my new chief (she depended on me), my family (I was a kid about to have a kid). How the hell had I let this happen?

On my way over to Keith's place that night, I stopped and bought three more pregnancy tests—just in case the last six had been false positives. Keith was lying in bed, so I took the opportunity to utilize the restroom. When I came back, I showed him the sticks. "I'm pregnant, Keith."

"Wow, Allie," he said. "That's awesome. Congratulations." He smiled at me like I'd just passed bunk inspection or some other mundane accomplishment.

Beyond that, the news of my pregnancy changed everything for the worse. If I thought I'd been ostracized before, I might as well have announced I had an incurable and highly contagious disease. My peers dropped me like a dead fish. My chief was so mad I thought for sure she was going to hit me; instead, she screamed me out of her office. Afterward, I stood in the passageway trying to catch my breath, silently pleading with myself not to cry. My dear friend Dre saw me from the top of the stairs, where she crossed her arms and shook her head. "Oh, you too?" I quietly asked.

"What the fuck, Al? What were you thinking? Haven't you ever heard of protection?"

Still others, both peers and supervisors alike, suggested I "get rid of the problem." They were counting on me to be ready to deploy. For a hot minute, I did consider aborting, thinking it might somehow regain for me the tiniest sliver of respect. But at the end of the day, while I support a woman's right to choose, I cherish all human life and already believed my baby was a part of me. She was a miracle, a dream of mine that happened to have been created much sooner than desired, but a dream nonetheless.

So, everyone was mad and I was young and scared. I apologized more than I ever have in my life, and of course internalized the entire ordeal as my fault alone. You worked so hard to advance in your career, you should have been more careful! For every inch I'd clawed forward in the Navy, getting knocked up set me back three feet. I wasn't sure I'd ever recover.

THE INTERNAL CRITIC

The thing about having a strong internal critic is that she

speaks louder than everyone around you. My whole life, I'd been a rule-follower and straight-edge successful. I'd never made waves or given anyone a reason—and thereby, the power—to judge me. When I turned out not to be the perfect sailor, though, no one was taking me seriously anymore. I'd broken the Navy's one unspoken rule right before we deployed, the biggest piece-of-shit thing you can do. I was forced to accept my imperfect nature. And in fact, that's all I could see about myself. I believed people were right to hate me. I hadn't just done a piece-of-shit thing; I was a piece of shit. The lowest of the low.

It would take me a long time to work through those feelings, to remember that I was, if not perfect, at least adequate—and still worthy of love. But I surely wasn't there yet, not by a long shot. The struggle to dig deep and find something about myself that I did not hate was excruciating, especially after Keith and I failed to work out. What finally would change for me was growing exhausted. I'd take in so many opinions from the cheap seats, letting everyone else tell me what I should or should not do, that after a while I just couldn't keep up anymore. But that was still a ways off. I had other mistakes to make before I got to that point.

Drowning in others' opinions of what I should and shouldn't do and who I should or shouldn't be, I no longer knew what Allie thought or wanted. In attempting to erase her imperfections, I'd effectively erased myself.

I had to learn to tune out the haters. We all have to learn this essential fact of life. There are so, so many of them—far more than the number of people who will support you through your darkest days. Their opinions are as fast and thoughtless as they are numerous. And they're fickle, subject to change.

You can't place your faith in something that precarious, because those opinions, they're like lead weights. If you grasp onto them while you're caught in the riptide, thinking they are a lifeline, you'll sink. Doing what other people want you to do won't save you. Those people aren't out in the water with you. They're not the ones who are pregnant, or peeing on sticks scared to death, or tasked with raising a baby alone. They've joined in with the naysayers hurling insults because it's easy. They're watching from the shore just to see if you will drown.

Fuck them. Quit keeping up with the Kardashians. Those people never mattered and they will not help you survive. Later, I'll talk more about my Circle of Trust—the friends and family whose opinions really do matter—but for now, just remember that life preservers are circular too, and they buoy up everyone: even the perfectly imperfect.

3

ON FINDING YOUR VOICE

I stayed on the USS Emory S. Land until I was twenty weeks pregnant, at which point I was transferred to my next duty station at Naval Base Kitsap. Whereas before I'd been attached to a ship, now I was attached to the base itself—specifically the administration building that housed the "top brass" (the commanding officer, the executive officer, and the command master chief). All three of their offices were on the top floor of the administration building. It was the kind of place where you walk in and your asshole puckers a bit because you know there's a high probability you'll run into someone important.

The day I reported, a chief (superior) welcomed me and another sailor who was checking in at the same time. He started shooting the shit with us about where we'd come from, ship life, the works. As I was rambling on about my time aboard the USS Emory S. Land, he abruptly stopped me mid-sentence. "You know what? It looks like you're assigned to the parking division here on base, but I think you're going to be a better fit somewhere else. Wait right there." He went upstairs for a bit, then came back and said, "I'm going to make you Command Master Chief's executive assistant (EA). It's a big job that requires you to be on the ball at all times, but I think you'd be great at it. How does that sound?"

It sounded like an honor, so I cheerfully accepted. Anything would be better than scrubbing debris off the hulls of small boats; plus, I'd be working directly for the military elite! I wondered hopefully, Could it be that my career isn't actually over, but just beginning? The chief told me that my position was conditional on Command Master Chief's approval. "But don't worry," he said. "This job requires a certain look, and you've got it." He then commended me on being well-spoken, but I almost didn't hear that compliment in my caught-off-guard response to his first comment.

Right away, I went upstairs to meet Command Master Chief (CMC). He was courteous and brief, asking multiple questions about my previous command and the skillsets I had acquired. He then gave me a once-over and dismissed me with a, "Congrats, the job is yours."

Just happy not to be stuck in a parking garage, I started the following day. It didn't matter that I'd never done any of what I was expected to do, besides answer a phone. I showed up determined to bust my ass, learn as much as I could, and overall kill it in my new role as the CMC's EA. There in the admin office, I saw for the first time other pregnant sailors. I noticed they'd all taken advantage of some of the allowances afforded to pregnant women in the military: for example, you can get a chit, or permission slip, from your doctor stating that your ankles are swollen, excusing you from wearing Navy-issue boots. I found this double standard unprofessional and decided to distance myself from those women by following dress protocol to a T. In all the ways that mattered, this new job felt like an opportunity for redemption. I wouldn't let anything get in the way of that salvation.

"YOU'RE FINE"

My first Command Master Chief was awesome. He taught me a lot, treated me well, and demanded my absolute best. Soon, though, he was offered a promotion that would place him in Japan, and he graciously accepted. The Navy identified his replacement, a Master Chief from a submarine, who could report in six months' time. In the meantime, Naval Base Kitsap appointed a Senior Chief who would assume the CMC role until it was properly staffed.

This Senior Chief was a frequent flyer in my office. We had a comfortable, casual rapport. He would always make it a point to stop by my desk and engage in back and forth banter. When he transitioned into his new role as acting Command Master Chief, however, and moved into the office next to my desk, things gradually began to change.

One day he was getting ready for a big meeting, and asked me to prepare a folder that included all of the relevant handouts and information. Right away I complied and ensured everything he would possibly need could be found in that bright yellow folder. Forty-five minutes later, he called the office screaming because I'd left out an important handout. He told me that it had made him look "like an idiot" in front of his peers and I needed to rectify the situation immediately. Having triple-checked the folder before he'd left, I knew I hadn't forgotten that handout—but biting my tongue, I apologized and promised to bring him another one right away. I called him from my cell phone when I arrived outside the building. "Hey," I said, "I'm here. Do you want me to come in?"

"No, I'll meet you outside."

He walked out to the parking lot and, apologizing again, I handed him the missing handout. "I'm so sorry, Senior Chief, I thought for sure I included this document."

He didn't bother to take it. Instead, he placed his hands tightly around my shoulders and pushed me against the government-issued car I'd been driving. He leaned so far forward, I could feel his breath on my cheek. "Don't you ever embarrass me like that again," he warned, before snatching the handout from my hands and quickly walking away.

Other incidents followed—often unpredictable, always unwarranted. Senior Chief would often do things to prove he was in complete control, like twist my arm behind my back and bend my wrist until I was on the floor begging for him to stop. It was as if he enjoyed the sight of me tapping out, begging to be freed, completely at his mercy.

Over time, the physical abuse turned sexual. He began to demand that I stand next to him, on his side of the desk, as we discussed the day's agenda. As we chatted about each item on his agenda, he would rub his hands up and down my butt and thighs, briefly brushing my crotch with his hands. "Senior Chief, stop," I'd say.

"Baby, baby," he'd whisper his pet name for me. "You're fine." He'd pull me closer as I'd inch away, slowly losing my military bearing.

"No, seriously, please don't do that," I'd reiterate.

He'd inevitably respond by slapping me on the ass. "It's just a joke," he'd huff.

"Well, it's not funny," I'd say, quickly exiting his office.

This turned into a regular occurrence, until one day I had simply had enough. I was angry, I was uncomfortable, I was scared, and I needed help. I decided to find a close friend of mine who happened to be higher ranking than me. I thought if I could confide in her about the fire I was currently walking through, she would steer me in the right direction.

After doing a quick sweep of my building, I finally found her in a quiet office two floors away from where my abuser sat. I closed the office door, and through tears, I word-vomited everything that had been taking place in my work space. I walked her through the inappropriate jokes, the physical and mental abuse, and the regular sexual contact that was occurring. After listening to my story, she looked me dead in the eye and said, "I'm sorry this is happening to you, Allie, I am. I wish I could take this from you—but I can't. Welcome to being a woman in the military. It's just the way things are. It's unfair, but there's absolutely nothing you nor I nor anyone else can do about it."

Because she'd been in the Navy a lot longer than I had, I

took her at her word. I knew it wasn't right to treat anyone like that, but her words made this junior sailor feel powerless. I'd reported it and been told the only option I had was to deal with it. So I did. The military does not operate under the same rules as civilian life. If you're getting assaulted at your place of work, there is no HR, no finding a new job; you are contractually bound never to leave your post unmanned. There is no switching offices, no safe place to run to; you are stuck where you're at until you've fulfilled your designated time.

In other words, you're fucked.

As time went on, so did the abuse. Sadness, anger, terror, shame, and disgust haunted my every move. I began deflecting my feelings onto those I loved. Although I felt defeated and discouraged, I knew I had to give reporting one last solid try. I made the decision to go to someone even higher-ranking than my friend, a chief I knew and trusted. I sought him out one day and told him everything that was occurring in my work place. After I was through reporting, all the chief could muster up was that he'd "talk" to Senior Chief about his behavior. Then he walked away.

Senior Chief ignored my existence for several days after that, which I preferred over enduring his abuse. When he finally broke his silence, he did so with a straightforward question: "Do you know how many women have reported me?"

"No, Senior," I sheepishly replied.

"Several. And do you know what's been done about it?"

"No...I don't."

"Nothing!" He stood up and crossed his arms as if to mock me and say I'm still here.

It was in that moment that I realized I was on my own. There were no lifeboats coming to save me or whimsical lighthouses to guide me to shore. I was alone in the depths, treading water and taking the waves, anxiously awaiting the day our new Command Master Chief reported for duty.

UNDRESSED

Eight weeks after giving birth, I went back to work. Nothing had changed in my absence; Senior Chief picked up where he'd left off with the same repulsive behavior. The fear I had day in and day out walking into work was tangible. It was as though I was living in an unending horror film with no way out.

The abuse reached its peak one sunny afternoon when

Senior Chief didn't stop at rubbing my thighs and touching my ass. He followed it up with a sudden shove to my chest, which forced my back onto his desk. He proceeded to forcefully spread open my legs and began dry-humping me through our uniforms. He was 240 pounds and I was 120 pounds soaking wet. It was so unexpected, and it happened so fast, that I was caught off-guard with no time to react. I pleaded for him to stop, eventually managing to get away. I was shaking and crying and angry and ashamed.

I decided to create some space between myself and my work environment by vacuuming the entire staircase that led to my office. One of my peers who was above me in rank, a yeoman second class (YN2), recognized me vigorously handling the vacuum and intervened by trying to spark a mundane conversation.

"Morning, Haz."

"Morning, YN2."

"Haz, I heard the gossip about duty sections and your job again this morning," he said as he rolled his eyes.

"Yup, because I report to the acting Command Master Chief, people think my job is glamorous, like I'm privileged just to breathe the same air as him. I wish I could just catch my breath, people just don't get it."

His eyes grew wide, and I realized he'd bought into the general consensus that because I worked for the higher-ups, I was like some golden child of the base who got everything handed to her.

The vent session continued for a few moments as I casually explained everyday life in my office, including the abuse that continuously occurred. The things that were happening to me had become so routine that when I spoke of them it was like I was talking about the weather. So casual, so insignificant, so normal. Our conversation came to a halt when we were abruptly interrupted by a group of young sailors headed in our direction.

"I better get back to vacuuming, YN2," I quietly said as I turned away.

"Hey, Haz...I'm here, ya know, if you need me."

I nodded my head as I went back to vacuuming, intent on forgetting it all as quickly as possible.

Later that day, I was working at my computer when I heard the admin chief's voice outside my office. "Haz?" I looked up from my computer screen and saw him standing in the doorway.

"Yes, Chief?"

Rather than reply, he motioned for me to follow him. I removed my CAC card from the card reader and followed his lead. My mind began to race. Had I done something wrong? Was I in trouble? Internally, I reviewed every email I'd sent that day and every duty I'd checked off my to-do list. The twenty-second walk to his small, private office seemed like a fifteen-minute mile.

As I stepped inside, Chief asked me to shut the door. I knew then that my fate was sealed. Somewhere along the line of today's events, I'd royally and seriously fucked up. He took a seat on top of the vacant desk closest to me, leaving one foot dangling off the side. I stayed standing, uncomfortable and confused, as I waited to be undressed. Not literally—when someone gets "undressed" in the military, it means they're getting their ass chewed. Chief looked me dead in the eye and began to speak in a stern yet concerned voice. "I need you to answer me honestly, Haz. How long has all of this been going on?"

Unlocking my gaze from his, I stared at the wall. "Chief, what are you talking about?"

Raising his voice an octave higher, he asked again, "Haz, how long?"

"I have no clue what you are talking about, Chief, but I do know I need to get back to work." As I turned away from him, completely out of character and showing zero regard for his rank—the admin chief shouted and a tear effortlessly slipped out of my eye.

"Haz, get back here and take a seat. This conversation is not done until I say it's done." He slid the chair next to me away from the desk. I slipped into it and buried my head in my hands.

"How long?"

I sat there in silence for what seemed like hours, Senior Chief's voice playing over and over in my head. Do you know how many women have reported me? I'm still here.

Finally, I mustered up the courage to speak. "Just before I had the baby. What started off as snide comments and inappropriate pet names slowly turned into physical altercations." I paused before going further, and in that instant my timidity flared into fury. "Why do you even care, Chief? It's the good ol' boys' club anyway, right? I'm going to give you all this information, and you're going to sweep it under the rug and it's never going to go anywhere. That's what's happened the last two times I've tried." I sighed and threw my hands in the air. "You know what? It's fine, I'm fine, everything's fine. Let's just go back to work and forget this conversation ever happened." I crossed my arms beneath my chest and waited for the shakedown I knew was coming.

Chief slowly shook his head and cleared his throat. "Haz, I can't do that. I don't know what kind of club you think I'm a part of, but there is no broom and there is no rug. I already have some idea of how it happened. I'm a chief, I hear things. Now what I want is to hear your side of the story."

Suddenly, I recalled the conversation I'd had with the YN2 by the stairs. The puzzle pieces began to fall into place. "If I tell you," I said, "will you be satisfied and not report it? Senior Chief will know it was me."

"I have to report it whether you come forward or not," he admitted.

I felt trapped! Crying and battling my fight-or-flight reflexes, I stared at my hands. Chief said, "Let's head down to Mr. Bruce's office (our department head at the time) and get this done in one shot."

"Okay."

I wiped my tears and stood up. The admin chief opened the door and ensured I exited first. He was following my lead this time around, as if he knew I was going to change my mind and bail at any moment. I didn't, though. Instead, I found my voice. I told leadership the whole story, and when I was done, the chief called Senior Chief (who was still the acting CMC) and told him he was needed at the judge advocate general's (JAG) office. He spun it like a sailor was in trouble, so he wouldn't be suspicious. That's where they relayed the allegations being leveled against him, and informed him that the Naval Criminal Investigative Service (NCIS) would be carrying out a full investigation.

TOWARD THE SURFACE AND THE LIGHT

Speaking up requires bravery and determination when no one hears you, but the first time someone actually does hear you changes everything. Before the admin chief heard me out, I'd given up on ever being taken seriously. I'd accepted that my treatment at the hands of Senior Chief really was just "life as a woman in the Navy." Once he nudged me, though, no one could shut me up again. From that point on, I made the decision that I was never going to allow anyone else to tell me something was acceptable and right, when it was so clearly what I knew to be wrong.

"Allie's too fat," they said. "Allie, you'll never make it through boot camp. Allie, you should have an abortion." No, no, and no. Not only had I slimmed down and made it through boot camp, I'd since made rank twice, making E5 in three years. I'd also had a beautiful baby girl who gave me purpose and life.

I stopped taking what other people told me as the gospel truth, and finally found my own voice. I quit opting for what was easy, and started fighting for what was true and morally right. Would it have been a lot easier for me to just tell the admin chief that he was way off-base and leave it at that? Hell yeah. But I didn't, and standing up for myself changed the entire course of my life. I wasn't going to bend over and take it anymore—not at work and not outside of work.

At some point, you're going to have to fight the good fight, which will also be the hard fight. And you're likely going to do it alone. I got lucky that I had an incredible admin chief on my side, but until that point, and later on the witness stand, it was just me. No other lifeboat was coming. Every time I opened my mouth to speak, it was like I swallowed more water. There was an ocean of people surrounding me, all with their own agendas, who wanted me silenced because it was better for them.

I wasn't believed when I reported my rape at the gym. My peers and leaders failed to take action when I reported Senior Chief's unacceptable behavior. Under all that water, I couldn't get a word in edgewise until I demanded that I be heard. By then, there was no decision to make. I could have stayed silent, and I would have stayed exactly where I was—maybe even sinking a little deeper. But I kicked back up toward the surface and finally found myself out of the depths of darkness, and in the security of the light. You've got to get back up. You've got to keep going, you've got to keep speaking, YOU HAVE GOT TO TAKE YOUR POWER BACK!

That said, there's a time for acceptance, too. So let's talk about that.

ON ACCEPTANCE

In the midst of everything happening in the Navy, I gave birth to my daughter Addisen. I was lucky in the sense that my whole pregnancy had been super easy. My weight had stayed in the expected range, the only consistent craving I'd had was a turkey sandwich, and I'd been able to keep working out. Therefore I had every reason to expect an easy delivery—the perfect start to my new life with my sweet baby, Addie.

The day before I went into labor, I was running wind sprints up a steep hill by my apartment. After my third or fourth sprint, I felt a sting of pain near my groin. It didn't feel right, so I slowed down and walked back home. I stayed off my feet for the remainder of the day. As the sun began its descent, I began to have contractions. By nightfall, they were in full effect.

Alone in my living room, I debated whether to call for help. I was leery of showing up at the hospital too early. What if it was just a false alarm? I settled on the couch and practiced my breathing exercises. Sleep was non-existent that night as I coached myself through waves of contractions.

As soon as the sun peered through my window, my phone rang. It was my mom. "Hey babe, how are you?"

Another contraction hit, and I couldn't answer.

"Al? Are you okay?"

"Yeah, I'm just—I think I'm having contractions—I'm not sure—it feels like cramps."

"Al, you're in labor. You need to get to the hospital!"

Luckily, I had a friend who lived right next to me. She showed up outside my house within moments and we made it to the Naval hospital in record time. Upon admittance, I was dilated to 9.5 centimeters and had high hopes my baby girl would arrive within the hour.

Thirteen hours later, I was still in the thick of labor. So much for high hopes.

Just when I thought I was on the brink of losing my shit,

the doctor told me it was time to push. I did. Nothing. I tried again. Nada. I pushed and pushed and pushed but we were making ZERO progress. My doctor was becoming increasingly impatient and worried. "Allie, you have twenty minutes. I'm starting the clock now. If you can't get her out in twenty minutes, we're going to have to take her by C-section," he said.

Umm, fuck that! My birthing plan specifically stated I wanted to deliver my baby naturally, so veering off-course wasn't an option.

Well, like most birthing plans, it all went to shit. In the end, I had a vacuum-assisted birth, meaning the doctor assisted my baby's transit through the birth canal by attaching a vacuum to her head. Yes, folks, my baby was literally sucked out of my vajayjay. We didn't have another option. Addie had been stuck in the birth canal for hours; she was at risk of oxygen deprivation, and by extension, brain damage.

She let out a howl of indignation when she arrived that let us know she was breathing just fine. However, there'd been a problem with the placement of the vacuum, and the procedure had de-scalped her partway. The top of her head was pulled back and hanging. The nurses quickly took her from my chest and ushered her out of the room, where they could determine the extent of the damage.

"Please go with her," I said to my mom, "just go with her and ensure she's okay." My mom kissed me on my forehead and quickly exited the room. Time seemed to stop as I anxiously awaited any sort of news about my daughter's health. My mind wandered to worst-case scenarios as my anxiety soared through the roof.

I was actively losing what was left of my sanity when the door to my room slowly creaked open. Through all the chaos, I saw my sweet baby girl wrapped snugly in a tiny pink blanket. She had sutures across the whole top of her head, but they assured me no permanent damage had been done. Thank you, Jesus! Seeing her de-scalped and wailing in pain was a trauma I will never forget, but her scar has since faded—reduced to the size of a penny.

I wish I could say I had reached the end of my birthing experience, but the chaos didn't stop there.

While the nurses were cleaning up my destroyed hoo-hah, one of them mentioned the amount of blood still exuding from "down there." When I questioned her about it, her concern morphed into a nonchalant attitude. "It's normal. We've just got to watch it. You will be just fine."

With my newly minted voice, I should have spoken up for myself right then and there, but I hadn't yet perfected that skill and I surely wasn't a medical professional! She said I would be fine, so I would be fine. I accepted that.

They discharged me the following day, reminding me to expect some bleeding. "If you pass any clots bigger than a quarter," the lead nurse cautioned, "come back."

"Okay, thanks," I agreed, my mind already elsewhere. The entire way home, I marveled over Addie's tiny features, her perfect toes, her button nose, her legs that she loved to move around. "From here on out, it's not about me anymore," I told her, smiling. "It's all about you, sweet girl."

CRANBERRY SAUCE

At home, life took on a new rhythm, one that revolved around diaper changes, nap times, and feedings. I made sure to take care of myself, too, which meant managing what seemed like an alarming amount of blood loss—but ostensibly no more than I'd been led to expect.

When the bleeding still hadn't stopped after several days, I went back to the Naval hospital. I described my condition to the nurse at the triage desk. She brushed me off and dismissed my concerns summarily, not bothering to do something as simple as a check-up. "Bleeding is normal," she reiterated. "What you are experiencing is normal."

I guess everything's okay, then, I thought—a line I continued to feed myself between feeding Addie and changing out my soaked sanitary pads every hour (TMI, I know). This trend continued for a solid week. The bleeding was persistent and failed to let up.

I returned to the Naval hospital again, hoping to get in front of a fresh set of eyes. Instead I was met by the same dismissive nurse. "Something doesn't seem right," I told her. "I'm really concerned about it. Can you just check me out?"

"You're fine. In fact, you're cleared to fly. Go enjoy your time with family and quit worrying. Your body is doing exactly what it should be doing."

I decided to fly home to Arizona. Losing copious amounts of blood had left me feeling faint and tired. I knew if I flew home, I could get help caring for Addie and maybe even some sleep. My first night at home, my parents threw a pizza party. They invited my aunt Deb and uncle Chad, as well as my cousin Montana, with whom I'd been close since childhood. We enjoyed catching up over pepperoni and sausage pizza and drooling over our family's newest addition.

After dinner, I started feeling poorly. I was cramping a lot, bleeding a lot, and getting dizzy every time I stood up. I went to lie down on my parents' bed, which was surrounded by plush white carpet. Montana followed suit, keeping me company, making me laugh when the pain became too much to bear. I thought I'd be okay until I suddenly felt something shift inside. "Oh my God, it's coming out!" I shouted. "OH MY GOD, Montana, grab a towel or something and put it over the carpet. I have to stand up."

Montana picked up the first towel she found and ran back to where I was standing. "What's coming out, Al? What's happening?" she asked, terrified.

But then she saw. Right there, all over my parents' pristine carpet, I passed a clot the exact size and appearance of a can of cranberry sauce, all firm and scarlet. (To this day, I can't eat cranberry sauce.) As soon as I delivered the impressively sized blood clot, blood began to gush out of me. Montana screamed for my mom, who came skidding to a stop at the doorway of what must have looked like a scene from a horror movie: blood, dark red blood, everywhere. Not hesitating for a second, my dad came in and scooped me up in his arms like I was still his little child, and rushed me out to his truck. "I'm taking her to the hospital," he said, fully in command. "Everyone else stay here and take care of Addisen."

The hospital admitted me right away. That's when I found

out the cause of the bleeding: a quarter of my placenta was still inside me, festering. A simple check at any one of the times I'd shown up at the hospital, complaining of pain and bleeding, would have revealed their mistake—but they hadn't bothered, and the consequences were severe.

NO MORE BABIES. EVER.

I spent the majority of my maternity leave in Arizona, shuttling between my parents' house and the hospital. I underwent multiple D&Cs (dilation and curettage, the procedure normally performed during an abortion) to clean out my uterus. Each time they were hopeful it'd be the last time, but I continued bleeding, and kept having to return for one procedure after another. After four or five of these operations, I was out of time and no closer to having any answers. I'd already been granted one extension to my maternity leave; now I had to return to Washington.

Back on base, I scheduled a follow-up appointment with my OBGYN. I brought my medical records and explained everything that had happened post-delivery. "I'm still bleeding, I'm still uncomfortable," I told him. "The civilian doc said my iron is scary low and I'm dizzy and tired most of the time. What can you do for me?"

"We'll need to take you to surgery one more time," he said. "I have to get in there to see exactly what's going on with your body and where this bleeding is coming from, so we can get it under control."

Willing and hopeful, I phoned my mom so she could fly out and watch the baby, and I went under anesthesia one more time. I awoke, at last, with a diagnosis: blistering infection, everywhere! Without getting into all the clinical details, the leftover placenta had basically rotted inside me and infected my many lady parts. They were so full of puss and infection that they hadn't been salvageable. While I was sedated, my doctor had performed a complete hysterectomy, including an oophorectomy. No uterus. No ovaries. No more babies. Ever.

"I'm so sorry," he told me when I was conscious enough to grasp the meaning of his words. "I wasn't able to save anything."

I'll remind you here that I was twenty-one years old. I was only just beginning to think of myself as a woman. One day I couldn't stop bleeding. The next, I would never bleed again. You can't menstruate without a uterus. While I was trying to wrap my mind around this, the doctor continued, "We'll give you an additional four weeks off-duty to heal and gain some strength back!" He quietly turned and left the room.

For months, I struggled against my own reality, refusing to accept the cold, hard truth. So much for my brood of multicolored seashell children. How was it possible that I would never bear any more babies? How could I feel like a woman again? How could I possibly feel whole again?

As my self-worth plummeted, I sank into depression. The pounding, stinging waves were pummeling me; I was being assaulted, physically and mentally, from every side. Underwater more often than not, I could no longer tell which way was up, or in which direction to chase the sun. Who was Allie, if not a woman?

I'll tell you. She was a sailor and a mother who had other responsibilities, who had pledged upon the birth of her daughter to always be there, no matter what—vowing that Addie, and not Allie, was the most important thing now.

So even though it was hard to forget about my own misfortune, I made sure it was harder to forget about her. I focused on the fact of her, her real and blessed existence. Never mind multiple children; some women struggle to even bear one. Remembering that made me grateful. I also worked to redefine womanhood, by celebrating all I had left, versus all I had lost. I still had breasts and hips and an ass that went on for days. My insides were fueled by a feminine spirit and my mind never lost sight of my fierce, womanly nature. Although my insides didn't make

it through that horrific ordeal, I did, and that was some-
thing I could put stock in.

ON PERSEVERANCE

Menopause is a bitch. Seriously, it's no fun.

Post-hysterectomy, my doctor warned me that I'd enter menopause fairly quickly. When your ovaries get surgically removed, there's no weaning off your hormones; withdrawal is instant, and your symptoms start almost immediately. I knew to expect hot flashes and night sweats—I just didn't know how bad they'd be.

The night before I woke up with my first true hot flash, I'd been crying about the fact that I couldn't have kids anymore. That gut-wrenching blow, plus the unnatural leaching of estrogen from my blood, had left me very emotional. Add to that the exhaustion of a first-time mother caring for a newborn. Meanwhile, I was beating back feelings of isolation and inadequacy. It was a lot to handle.

Even so, the emotional pain was nothing compared to my physical agony. In the wee hours of the morning, I awoke certain that my body was on fire. It felt like I was boiling from the inside out. Until that moment, I wouldn't have thought it possible for a human to be so hot—not even on the toughest runs during boot camp at high noon in August. I sat straight up in bed. Sweat poured from my skin in rivers. Just before my vision swam and I became nauseous, I caught the outline of a sweat angel on my sheets. I steadied myself against the edge of the bed and took deep, cleansing breaths, trying to cool off. Next I stripped off my clothes and stood naked in front of a fan. When that didn't work, I went outside. My apartment balcony overlooked the Puget Sound, and the night air, even in late summer, was crisp. Nothing but the breeze moved through the dark world around me. I threw up over the balcony railing, letting all that heat leave me in torrents. Then I sank to the concrete of my balcony and cried.

With the patio door open so I could hear Addisen in case she needed me, I bawled silent, wracking sobs, acutely aware of my aloneness. I was six months deep into the single parenting thing and angry because I was afraid. How am I going to get through this? I asked myself. The question would become a refrain. Even more terrifying was another question that plagued me: How could anyone ever love a woman so internally empty that she's hardly even a woman anymore? My inability to sleep through the night without sweating through my sheets was the first external sign of what had, to this point, been an entirely internal battle. No one can tell you've had a hysterectomy just by looking at you, but what man would share a bed with me now that I was pouring sweat all night long?

In your darkest hour, it's difficult to imagine the dawn. Had it not been for Addisen, I might have given up right then. Instead, slumped on my balcony at 3 a.m., I decided to dry the waterworks and quit feeling sorry for myself. If I was to be the mother she deserved, I'd have to focus on putting our lives back together, no distractions or excuses—especially not of the male variety. The only man who'd get my attention was Senior Chief, my former CMC, simply so that justice might be served.

THE NEW MA

The best laid plans, right? I really had sworn off dating, but the only thing harder to predict than how your court case will shake out is love.

I managed to pull myself together and was beginning to get the hang of being a single mother. One morning, as per usual, I went to the gym on base before work. After-ward, I showered and put on my uniform, then drove over to my office. As I was walking up to the building, a friendly E5 I'd never seen before opened the door for me. "Thank you, Petty Officer," I said, skirting past him and thinking *God, he's cute,* at the same time reminding myself *Forget it, Allie, he's off the table.*

The stairs that lead to my office were directly ahead of me. I started climbing them and with each step I cleared, I couldn't help but feel as though I was being followed or watched. Sure enough, when I turned around on the land-ing, he was staring up at me. "Can I help you?" I asked, a bit snippy.

"Yeah, uh, Where's the admin office?" he asked.

"It's directly to your left," I said, pointing the way.

"Thank you."

"No problem." I kept walking, but he never started. Even after I'd finished the whole next flight, he still stood at the bottom, arms crossed beneath his chest, watching me. His face was so kind, his eyes were so earnest, and his presence was so inviting that I couldn't help but to smile and laugh a little. He laughed, too, and continued on his quest to find the admin desk—the location of which, I later found out, he'd known the whole time.

A few weeks later, I was sitting in a meeting when my good friend and a member of my Circle of Trust, Amy Abbott, asked if she could speak to me privately. She was higher-ranking than me and a Navy cop to top it off. Although she was my friend, she wouldn't hesitate to call me out on my bullshit if I had done something wrong. As she began to speak I braced myself for the possibility of a lecture, but my worries turned into butterflies when she simply inquired if I had seen the new MA. (MA stands for master-at-arms, or Navy cop).

Puzzled, I quickly replied, "No, I don't think so."

"Hm. Well, his name is Sean Brazas. He asked about you earlier."

"Really?"

"Yeah. He asked me about the female with short curly hair who works upstairs. He thinks you're really cute and he wants to take you on a date. I know you have been through a lot recently, but I wouldn't be telling you this if I didn't think he was a chance worth taking."

The image of the E5 who had stood at the bottom of the

stairs hours earlier flashed through my mind. I felt a wave of excitement, but quickly reminded myself about the hell I was walking through. "Um, one, I don't even know this guy," I said, "and two, I have a ton of baggage I'm currently lugging around," I reminded Amy.

"Will you at least Facebook-stalk him with me?"

Without an ounce of hesitation, I replied, "Um, duh."

She giggled and pulled up his page. It was him all right.

"Sean Brazas. Huh."

"He's a K9 handler. He left today with his dog for a mission in New York," she said, "but he asked me to give you his phone number. He wants you to text him!"

"No way," I resisted. "I NEVER make the first move, that's the man's job."

Sneakily, Amy gave Sean my number instead. He texted that afternoon and didn't stop for three consecutive days. He then mustered up the courage to ask me on a date as soon as he returned home from New York.

I agreed, but cautiously, adamant that everything would be on my terms. No, he could not pick me up, I'd drive to his place. No, I would not come into his apartment, I would wait on the stoop while he gathered his wallet and hat. I did let him drive us to Whiskey Creek, a steakhouse just up the road, but that was the only request I gave in to.

It wasn't long before I let down my guard and relaxed, against my better judgment. I just couldn't help it. Sean was the easiest, most incredible man in the world to talk to. Our chemistry was instant and electric—truly a once-in-a-lifetime, soulmate kind of connection. At Whiskey Creek, we chatted over dinner from 9 p.m. until closing time, then we hit the road back to his apartment and talked in the parking lot for hours. As the Washington rain set in, we couldn't seem to wrap up our conversation. Every time we said goodbye, one of us would bring up something else, stalling our separation, until the drizzling rain turned into a downpour. "Okay, I really have to go now," I said, regret at parting already pooling in my heart. That's when Sean kissed me. It was the best smooch I had ever experienced; no amount of descriptive words could do it justice.

"Hey, Allie," he called as I walked back to my car.

"Yesss?" I said, gently but enthusiastically.

"I'm going to marry you one day."

Outwardly I replied with a Yeah, right eye roll and smile,

but inside I melted like butter. I drove away, knowing for a fact that I, too, would marry that man one day.

Ohhhh, fate.

HEAD HELD HIGH

Following my first date with Sean, things really started moving on the court case. All along, I'd been meeting with my lawyers—the JAG officers—and preparing for the day I'd actually take the stand against my former acting Command Master Chief. In mounting the evidence necessary to discredit a man of Senior Chief's rank, they'd looked into his military record and made some phone calls. They discovered that women had reported him for misconduct at a number of his previous duty stations. The Naval Criminal Investigative Service (NCIS) collected statements from those who were willing to talk. I wasn't privy to the details of their stories, but from what my lawyers hinted at, they were similar in scope to mine. Just knowing there were others, and that I wasn't alone, was powerful and created the momentum I needed to continue trudging forward.

The morning of the court-martial, the skies were gray and water drizzled from the sky. I couldn't help but feel like the weather fit the occasion. I felt nervous and jittery, scared about having to face Senior Chief again. I hadn't seen him since the day my admin chief had intervened. At the courthouse, I was told to wait in the witness room along with the other women who would be testifying in person. There were four of us, including a civilian woman with Down Syndrome who had worked in the base galley. We couldn't talk and our cell phones had been confiscated, so we alternately stared at the floor and at each other. I listened very closely to see if I could hear anything happening in the courtroom—the opening remarks, perhaps, or Senior Chief's lawyer talking to the judge. But all I could hear was silence, deafening silence.

When it was my turn to take the witness stand, I walked into battle with my head held high. I didn't want to look at Senior Chief, but as he was seated across from the witness stand facing the judge, eventually it was impossible to avoid and ignore his large stature. What I saw was a robot, a stone-cold shell of a man who'd completely checked his emotions at the door. He refused to look me in the eye, and I refused to do the same, which I suppose made it all a bit easier for both of us.

Eventually, I saw Sean enter the courtroom and slide into a pew next to our close friend, Matt Nalley. Matt was a senior MA who was present during the trial in case Senior Chief's sentence included a trip to the brig (military jail). If it did, Matt would escort Senior Chief in handcuffs to where he belonged, behind bars. Having Sean in the courtroom gave me eyes to stare into and a safety net to cling to as I continued to answer question after question about how I'd fallen victim to Senior Chief's disgusting games.

As I pleaded my case, I remember less about how things actually proceeded, and more about how they made me feel. Try proving to a room full of doubters that yes, you really were sexually assaulted, and no, you didn't like it. It's humiliating. It's also super hard to keep calm, control your anger, and stick to "just the facts" when the other side is doing its best to make you look like an incompetent liar accusing an innocent man of heinous crimes.

I do recall with perfect clarity the moment when Senior Chief's lawyer lost the case for him. He and his lawyer were trying to make it seem like I'd invited his attention, but unfortunately for Senior Chief, his lawyer hadn't done his homework. "So, Petty Officer (I'd recently been promoted)," the lawyer said, pacing before me, "you mean to tell me that come December, you were, in your words, 'terrified' of this man after he'd committed these alleged physical and sexual acts?"

"Yes, sir."

"If you were so 'terrified' of this man, then please explain to the court why you BEGGED to sit by him and his wife at the Naval Base Kitsap Christmas party. Your claims are contradicting and don't make sense."

"Well, sir," I responded, frankly dumbfounded, "you're right: that doesn't make sense—for the primary reason that I wasn't at the Christmas party. I wasn't even in Washington at the time the Christmas party took place; I was in Arizona with my family. Not only did I not do that, but I would never do that—and I have the documentation to prove it."

I looked—really looked—at Senior Chief then, my accusations giving way to questions. Why are you doing this? I asked with my eyes. Where did you think all the lying would land you? He just put his head in his hands. It was like he finally understood that he wouldn't be getting away with it, not this time, not against me and all the other women who weren't about to back down. If I had been at that Christmas party, Lord knows it would have been much harder to prove his guilt, if for no other reason than his rank gave him authority. He could, and probably would, have made up anything to save face, but he'd messed with the wrong girl, and come up with the wrong web of lies.

Later, back in the witness room, I sat down across from my comrade with special needs—a woman who'd reported Senior Chief before me, only no one had believed her. I felt so sad over the way he'd abused her, but also justified, as though she'd lent my story purpose. This is why it happened to me, I thought. This is why I'm here. God knew I was strong enough to follow through, to demand legal justice and not let my own, or these other women's claims, be swept under the rug. In that moment, I no longer cared whether we won or lost. What was important was that we'd persevered, and in so doing, had validated each other. Together, we'd established an unacceptable pattern of behavior in a high-ranking member of a male-dominated group. The jury might not believe us, but we knew what we'd been through, and soon the world would, too.

DIAMONDS IN THE ROUGH

After everyone had said their piece, we were dismissed so the jury could deliberate. Soon, my JAG officer called me to let me know they'd reached a verdict, and I returned to the courthouse with Sean by my side. Since Sean was a cop, he'd wanted to volunteer to be one of the men alongside MA1 Nalley on court duty in case Senior Chief was given brig time, but I'd convinced him it was a conflict of interest. "All right," he'd said, grudgingly, "then at least I'm going for you." We walked into the courthouse together, and he sat there holding my hand as the verdict was read.

Senior Chief was found guilty of several counts of sexual

misconduct. He received a reduction in rank from E8 (senior chief) to E1 (seaman recruit—what you enter the Navy as). He lost his retirement, which was significant as he had twenty-plus years of service, and was dishonorably discharged. He didn't get brig time, but he was made to register as a sex offender, a punishment that will follow him the rest of his life. While I can only speak for myself and not the other women involved in the case, I was satisfied with the outcome. I've never seen him again, nor has he tried to contact me.

People talk about "diamonds in the rough"—valuable people, places, and things that at first glance don't appear to be worth much. They might be ugly, or difficult, or ordinary on the outside, but the rock obscures the gem inside. My experience with the court-martial was like that geode. At first, it seemed insurmountable. I reported Senior Chief three times before anything was done about it, and even then, the odds of successfully bringing him to trial were long. Several other women, and more who would not or could not speak up, got their hands dirty trying to crack his side of the story. It took all of us to get it done. If any one of us had given up, we never would have been rewarded with the cool, crystalline truth. Senior Chief would never have gotten his just desserts, and we'd all still be locked in private prisons of grief and despair, questioning whether it hadn't just been in our heads. No. We cut to the heart of the matter, the diamond inside. And it turns out, diamond is harder than rock.

Sometimes you have to wade through shit, as one bad thing happens after another. People hurt you. They take sides. They don't believe you. It stinks to high heaven. Other times, you're up against a monster—a man, a debt, a disease—so big and bad that you're scared to even try to fight, and you let it consume you instead. That was me. Fortunately, I was able to take it all back—my self-esteem and my sexuality. Sean, Matt, Amy, my good friend Tara, and all those women helped me push through, and allowed me to reclaim the truths that I am lovable and worthy. Because I gave Sean a chance, I found my soulmate. Because those sailors and I stuck together, there's one less predator on the streets tonight.

It's like when you're sitting in traffic, and the light's taking too long to change. There's always that jackass who swerves out into another lane and takes the long way around, just so he doesn't have to wait at the light anymore. Had he waited thirty more seconds, the light would have changed and he could have gone straight home. But he grew impatient with the process. He gave up. He couldn't persevere. And now he's at the back of the pack.

I see the same thing with runners, because I am one.

You're running, making record time, and really feeling yourself. Then you hit that hill, the one with the thirty-degree incline, and you quit because it's too hard, you can't see the top. Little did you know the finish line was a mere 400 meters away. You miss experiencing the awesome thing—the victory, the pride, the accomplishment—all because you quit less than a mile too soon.

Call it your diamond in the rough, your traffic light, your road race; it doesn't matter. Just keep on treading water. When you give up out at sea, you sink, and when you sink, you miss the beauty of the sunrise. Sunrises have a way of making the world new again, imbuing it with strength and hope, reminding you to love yourself as you would love others. Never quit, never sink, and never miss a sunrise.

ON SELF-COMPASSION

When the court-martial happened, Sean's and my relationship was new and fresh. We'd only been dating for a few weeks. I didn't expect to have to give him an ultimatum so early into our relationship, but that's how it went. It had to do with kids; or rather, my inability to bear them.

On our very first date, I'd made the decision to tell Sean about my hysterectomy. I wasn't thrilled about divulging such personal information to a man I was just getting to know, but if he was going to take issue with it, I wanted to know right then, versus months down the road.

"Sean, I want you to know that I'm extremely interested in you. This night—this dinner—this date—have been nothing short of incredible. However, I want to be upfront with you straight out of the gate: I have had a complete hysterectomy. If that's a dealbreaker, I understand."

"What? No!" he exclaimed, immediately encouraging. "It's okay. We all have our own shit to bear, and your shit would never cause me to walk away."

PHEW! I thought to myself, This man is a keeper.

Fast-forward a month. Sean and I were in the middle of another fantastic date. As he poured me a glass of my favorite red wine, I couldn't believe my luck at having found this guy: a real one-of-a-kind gem. His positive outlook was contagious. Our chemistry was insane. Leaning closer to him, I said, "I'm so glad you're so accepting of the fact that I can't have kids. That's super rare, and I really appreciate it."

Sean stopped mid-pour and gave me a look of confusion. "Babe, what do you mean you can't have kids? Do you know this for sure?" he asked, semi-smiling, trying his best to keep it together.

"I am positive that I can't have any more kids. I told you that on our first date, handsome. Hysterectomy, remember?"

"Oh, that's right." Sean looked chastened. "To be honest, I really wasn't sure what all that meant. I just knew you'd had some sort of surgery and you seemed anxious while you told me about it."

Oh, my God, I thought to myself. "To be fair, after I told you, your response seemed absolute. You looked and sounded as if you knew exactly what I was talking about."

"I should have asked you what you meant and for that I am sorry," he acknowledged.

My shoulders slumped. I pulled back from him, crushed. "Is that a dealbreaker for you?"

"I-I-I don't know. Look, I really love you, Al. I have enjoyed every second we have spent together. But I need some time to think this over. I'm sorry. I'm so sorry."

"I understand," I said, a brave face obscuring my devastation and shame. "Just let me know what you decide."

"I will."

Sean and I wrapped dinner up, hugged and kissed good-bye, and I sobbed the entire way home.

HIS CHOICE

Self-compassion wasn't something I had in spades in those days. If I'd hated my "imperfect" body in middle school, by twenty-two, I thought I'd more or less given up the ghost. What use was I to anyone, broken as I was? Of course it had all been too good to be true. Why would a guy like Sean want a less-than-woman like me—especially when his personality, charm, and humor could land him any other girl in the world?

These were my thoughts in the week following our revelatory conversation. It was the longest and most painful week of my life. For seven straight days, "Stronger" by Kelly Clarkson became my anthem. Everywhere I drove, people could bet their bottom dollar that I'd be blaring that song and singing it at the top of my lungs. It was pathetic.

Sean and I hadn't spoken in a week when I ran into him at our base's PFA (Personal Fitness Assessment). As I was scheduled to be the PFA instructor that day, I showed up painfully early and leaned sleepily against the gym's brick wall so I could chow down on my breakfast bar in peace. I had just taken my first bite when off in the distance I heard a familiar voice: "Alllllliiiieeeee."

I turned toward the voice and saw Sean walking my way.

"Ssssseeeeeaaaannn," I called back.

Sean hustled down the hall and reached in for a hug. I opened my arms wide as he embraced me and held on tightly for several seconds. He leaned on the same brick wall mere inches from me and began to sneak pieces of my bar. We chatted back and forth about our week and brought each other up to speed on all we had missed. I was puzzled by this interaction, confused about why we were acting as if the entire hysterectomy conversation had never happened, and as if we hadn't just spent the week in silence.

Sean shot winks and flirtatious expressions my way throughout the entire PFA, and gave me one last bear hug once it was over. Afterward, I called Amy Abbott, my friend and confidant who had gotten us together. "I can't believe this," I word-vomited into the phone. "I never should have let him in. We never should have Facebook-stalked him. I should have shut it down from the start. I was finally beginning to be okay with the whole hyster-ectomy ordeal, then this incredible soul comes waltzing into my life. Now I'm going to lose him over something that's completely out of my control, something I can't fix."

Amy listened attentively, and assured me everything was going to work out in the end. "Sis, the guy comes into my office daily and asks me about you. He's not going anywhere. Just give him some time." Her words were encouraging, but I was the furthest thing from hopeful.

The weekend after the PFA, Bridget (my childhood best friend) came out to Washington to visit me. Prior to the shit hitting the proverbial fan with Sean, my friend Faivre had offered to watch Addie for the night so Bridget, Sean, and I could hit the town. Despite my misgivings, Bridget still wanted to meet Sean and see what all the hype was about. "Call him! Call him! Call him!" she chanted.

"Okay, okay, I'll call him. But I make ZERO promises he will actually show up."

With my heart pounding a million beats a minute, I hesitantly called his phone. "Hey, it's me." Duh. "Remember how I told you my best friend Bridget was coming into town and you had planned on meeting her?"

"Yeah, that's this weekend, isn't it?" he asked.

"Yes, that's this weekend. Anyway, I know things have been weird between us lately, but we still plan on going out tonight and I wasn't sure if you'd still want to come."

"Absolutely," he said. "Why don't we just meet at my house and go from there?"

"Sure! Sounds great!"

We ended up having a great night together—so great, in

fact, that Bridget and I crashed at Sean's house afterward. When I woke up the next morning in a hungover haze, I looked around the room, and then at a sleeping Sean next to me. Shit-shit-shit-shit-shit. You allowed him to do the one thing you said you wouldn't: have his cake and eat it, too. What a wishy-washy son of a gun. I began to gather my things.

A few moments later, Sean rolled over. All sleepy and sweet, he greeted me with a "Hey, gorgeous" that swelled my heart. "I had an awesome night with you and Bridget," he said. "I've missed you."

I stopped listening at that point because everything hurt— my heart, my soul, my head. I cut him off. "Sean, I love you and miss you and I want nothing more than us to go back to normal. I've waited over a week for you to make up your mind. I'm not going to do this half-in, half-out bullshit. To put it simply, it's unfair. I mean, God, have you even begun to do any sort of research on other ways we can have kids? Surrogacy? Adoption?" Frustrated, I crossed my arms under my chest and awaited his response.

Lying on his bed with his hands behind his neck, watching the blades of his ceiling fan spin around and around, he shrugged his shoulders. "No, I haven't done any research," he admitted, "and no, I haven't figured it out yet. I'm sorry, Al, I am!"

"I deserve so much better than a guy who doesn't know if he wants me or not due to something that happened TO me, something I didn't get a say in. I am caring and compassionate and hard-working and loving and driven and in shape and I've got a sweet little girl just waiting for her mommy to walk through the door and pick her up. I—we—are a steal, uterus or not, and if you can't see that, I think I have my answer.

"BUT, just so you know," I continued, "you could find a girl whom you love very deeply later on down the road, one who has all the 'parts' necessary to bear a child. And, Sean, she STILL may not have the ability to conceive. Naturally conceiving a child is not a guarantee for anyone. Hell, you might not be able to have kids. Your sperm might just not be with it. In which case, you'll have missed out on our opportunity for no reason. So, just so we are clear, the second I walk out that door, I am never coming back. There are no do-overs, no 'I'm sorrys,' and there are absolutely no take-backsies.

"So I'm going to ask you right here, right now, to choose. Either you want to be with me or not. I refuse to stand by while you sort out your shit."

Sean seemed stunned. For a minute, he didn't say a word. My heart began breaking in a million different pieces as I stood up and grabbed my things and headed toward his bedroom door.

"No, wait," Sean yelled as he grabbed me. "Fuck it. I'm okay with it. I love you more than I ever thought I could love someone. We can figure out kids when and IF we ever decide that we want more. But I can't lose you, Allie, I just can't. This week was torture, and I'm sorry that it took so long for me to come to this conclusion."

Shortly after the day of ultimatums, Sean moved in with Addisen and me, and the three of us became inseparable. After all the surgeries, all the assaults, all the court drama, I was finally happy. I finally felt complete.

Sean never once looked back. I wish I could say the same.

ONLY ROADBLOCKS

This was late August 2011. Even though I was fresh off my victory over Senior Chief, his conviction hadn't overturned my own guilt. I blamed myself for the sexual assaults I'd suffered both at his hands and those of John at the gym. I wondered, Did I ask for it in some way? Could I have stopped them earlier? What if I had yelled "no" more loudly? How many other women has John hurt since? How many women didn't—or couldn't—come forward about Senior Chief?

He had a family, a wife and kids. Although the court-martial had been a win for other women, it sure hadn't been for his wife. Because of his sex offender status, they'd had to sell their house, which was by a school, and move. He'd been demoted back to the galley, or cafeteria, on a separate base, until his dishonorable transition out of the Navy was complete. He may have ruined my life, but who was I to ruin his family?

Even as I struggled with these thoughts, I blamed myself further for the simple fact of being with Sean. He was the most amazing guy I had ever met, and while yes, he'd chosen me, perhaps I wasn't the best fit for him. I mean, I couldn't even have kids. Sean at least deserved the option to have them. Was it selfish of me to ask him to give that up? You suck, I told myself. It's your fault. It was always your fault. Forget about the goddamn bar. You're not even worth the running start.

Here I was with everything I could have wanted, and all I could see was what my choices had cost other people.

Sean, recognizing that I couldn't love myself during this period, loved me harder. He became the metaphorical pole that, even if I still couldn't clear the bar, would launch me that much closer, lifting me up and wrapping me in love. Any time I had to go to the hospital for another two-hour iron infusion, he'd come sit with me and play games to keep me entertained. If we brought Addisen, he'd chase her around the room until she was laughing so hard she couldn't breathe, then put her on his shoulders and do victory dances for me. There were tickle wars and heartfelt hugs for Addisen and me both, from the most doting boyfriend and would-be father you've ever seen. In every way, Sean not only accepted the fact that I was sick, but he tried to make it fun—to lighten the mood and in so doing, my life.

Of course, every infusion reminded me why I was sick; made me think of the blood, the nurse's denial, and ultimately, my hysterectomy. Whenever I thought about the future, I would get sad imagining a family with Sean that did not include a baby: that living manifestation of how much love we had for each other. Automatically, Sean would remind me, "You know what? There's adoption. We can get donor eggs and use a surrogate." He turned all of my mountains into molehills, and never stopped encouraging me. "You have to stop blaming yourself, Allie. Stop hating yourself. Forgive the past. Forgive yourself."

We all have to stop blaming ourselves. I, and perhaps you, too. Stop hating yourself, and forgive the past. Pull back and recognize that the things you thought would be the end of the world turned out to be only roadblocks, tiny obstacles with many available detours around them. Not everything is your fault; shit happens. You don't have control over all of it. Nobody does.

I was playing the role of villain. I had to retire that role and let go of a past I didn't choose for myself. I needed to be free to move forward and hold onto the "poles" in my life—whether internal or external, tangible or otherwise—that could lift me up and carry me to a better place.

When we stop judging ourselves with a critical eye, and instead see ourselves through the eyes of those who love us, we are instantly and honestly made more perfect. Not Perfect-with-a-capital-P perhaps, but certainly worthy of the love being shown to us. Flawed, my friends, but still. so. worthy.

YOU AND ME

On Valentine's Day 2012, I was getting an iron transfusion at the hospital. As I sat there with an IV in my arm, Sean and Addisen were playing Go Fish and acting silly. Amongst the chaos, Sean ever so casually looked over at me. "After this, we're going to drop Addisen off at your friend Hope's house, and I'm going to take you on a date."

"Just the two of us?"

"Just you and me, Al."

A few hours later, we were waving goodbye to Addie, and Hope was yelling after us, "You guys have a great time. Stay out as long as you'd like."

Sean took me back to Whiskey Creek, the restaurant where we'd had our first date. We had a typically amazing dinner, then hung around the table for a while just talking. I was madly in love with the greatest man I'd ever known and spent most of the evening staring into his eyes. Just as I was about to ask the waiter for our check, Sean cleared his throat and looked at me directly, his hands shaking and his voice cracking. He got down on one knee and began to speak, "The day I met you, I told you I was going to marry you, and I meant it, Allie Marie. Will you marry me?"

"OMG! YES! YES! I love you so much," I said through tears.

Although we'd been dating for a relatively short period of time, my faith in us—if not in myself—was unshakable. Sean was my soulmate, my partner through many lives, from time immemorial. I knew it then, and I know it now.

The restaurant brought out a nice bottle of wine. Its patrons cheered and clapped. We toasted to our future and all that it promised.

Rewind to Thanksgiving Day 2011. Sean had been notified

that he and his K9 would be deploying to the Middle East in April. Since the day he'd received the news, we'd been counting every precious second. A red-blooded American badass, Sean was as pumped to go fight in Afghanistan as he was sad to leave Addie and me behind. After all, it's what we'd signed up for: to serve our country and its interests. Romantic love, predestined as it may have been, came second to the call of duty.

In the months before Sean shipped out, he began to get emotional off and on about leaving us and the timing of it all. It wasn't that he didn't want to go; it was more about his love for us and all he'd miss while he was away. We planned to get married upon his return. The intervening months would give us time to save up to throw the fairy-tale wedding we both desired.

As part of his pre-Afghanistan checklist, Sean met with JAG officers and our good friend Chief Nalley to write his will. It was then that the gravity of where he was going and the danger that it represented set in. He came home from the meeting and had hardly made it through the doorway before he began to speak to me. "Listen, I really think we should get married now. If anything happens to me over there, I want to make sure you and Addisen will be okay—that you both will be taken care of. And I can't do that if we're not married. The benefits don't apply to fiancées."

"Nothing's going to happen to you, Sean," I insisted. "Babe, you deserve a big wedding with all your family and friends in attendance. If we do it now, no one's going to be there to witness it."

"I get that," Sean said, "and I feel the same. What if we keep things hush-hush and just get married at the courthouse, in secret? Then when I get home from deployment, we will throw the big wedding with all the fixings. It'll be great!"

"High five, babe! You TOTALLY knocked this one outta the park," I said with excitement.

On March 3, 2012, amongst a handful of our close friends and work family, we tied the knot.

My beloved left for training in New York later that month. From there he went to California, then Yuma, and finally to Afghanistan, landing in-country on May 1, 2012. Sean took my heart with him when he left, but in its place he left his love—and a burgeoning sense of self-compassion that on hard days allowed me to show myself kindness, the way that he always did, and would still want me to today.

What I didn't know then, but came to learn soon enough, was that the man who kissed away my fears and filled me with courage, strength, and unwavering love, would never step foot on American soil again.

ON GRIEF

The day before Sean died felt unusually long, though it was nothing compared to the days that would follow. I hadn't slept well all week, kept awake by lingering thoughts of Sean and how he was holding up in the fields of Afghanistan. He'd been kind enough to Skype with me every night before bed and call me every morning on my way to work up until May 24, the day his unit left on a mission outside the wire of his forward operating base (FOB). He warned me he wouldn't have a way to communicate for several days and told me not to worry.

Sean always shielded me from the horrors of his job there. When I'd ask how he was and how things were out there, he'd instantly reply, "It's really not too bad, babe, honestly." His reply was horseshit—we both knew it—and it always left my mind stringing together one worst-case scenario after another. As my sleep suffered, work started to wear me out. I couldn't help it; I missed him.

As the sun slowly left the sky on May 29, I still hadn't heard from Sean and I could no longer ignore the pit in my stomach. I was nauseous, emotional, and worried. Walking across the parking lot to my car after a full day's work, I was surprised to see my friend and fellow sailor Faivre sitting on a park bench near my parking space. "Hey," I said, plopping into the seat next to her. "Everything okay, Favs?"

"Yeah, fine. You?"

"Fuckin' terrible. I feel like ass, I haven't eaten in a few days, and I just can't shake this feeling that Sean's not coming home."

"I've been deployed numerous times," she reminded me. "Afghanis have horrible aim. They shoot a million times in a million different directions and cross their fingers that one measly piece of ammunition will hit us. Allie, look at me: Sean will be fine." She rubbed my arm encouragingly, but the tears were already falling.

"It's just such a strong, unshakeable feeling," I said. "But it's encouraging to know that their aim is shitty. Thanks for the pep talk, Favs. Lawd knows I needed it."

"Any time. If you need me, you call me," she demanded as I began to walk to my car.

In bed that night, I tossed and turned, restless and bracing myself for the worst. I tried everything to calm my anxiety, including a good old-fashioned self-scolding: You can't think this way for the entire time he's gone, Allie. It will be complete misery for you and for Addisen. Pull it together, mama. Sometime after midnight, I finally fell asleep, and by morning my fears had largely faded. Something about the blue skies and the sun beaming through my blinds seemed to promise better things. As I got ready for work, I wondered what Addie would be doing that day. She was out of town visiting family. I hoped she'd have a good day. I hoped I would, too.

MIL TO MIL

In the wake of the court-martial, the new Command Master Chief we'd so desperately been waiting for had reported to duty and taken over. He was a breath of fresh air for everyone who had fallen victim to Senior Chief's various assaults. He and I shared a strong professional relationship, and although my trust was hard to come by, especially with higher-ranking officials, Master Chief Peirsel was one of the few to eventually earn it.

On the sunny morning of May 30, 2012, I was tasked with

running an errand to the Naval hospital to pick up some posters that we needed for our lactation room. On my way there, I decided to phone Master Chief, in case he'd forgotten I wouldn't be in at my usual time.

Answering on the third ring, his voice sounded hesitant. "Haz?"

"Good morning, Master Chief!" I replied cheerfully. "I'm calling to remind you that I'm running that errand to the Naval hospital, so I won't be in for a while."

"Oh, o-okay," he said. "Haz, just make sure you go straight to the office after you're done, no pit-stops."

"Yeah, for sure. Master Chief, what's going on? You don't sound like yourself. Have I done something? Are you okay?"

"Yeah. Yeah, I'm okay. And no, you're fine. I'll just see you when you get here," he awkwardly announced, immediately hanging up the phone.

"FUCK!" I yelled, to absolutely no one but myself. "What could I have possibly done to upset him?"

I pondered that question the entire five miles to the Naval hospital.

After picking up the posters, I headed back to base. While driving, I called Favs to apologize for my pessimism the evening before. "Hey," I greeted her, "I just want to let you know that I wasn't myself last night. I was being completely pessimistic. Your words are the only ones I should allow to occupy my mind. Sean will be fine!"

"Where are you?" she asked, almost cutting me off mid-sentence.

"I'm just about to pull through the gate. So I have to let you go soon, sista."

"Do me a favor, Al. Stay by your car once you park. I'm almost on base, too. I had a really bad night, and I need someone to talk to."

"Sure, but I'm already late and Master Chief sounded off this morning. So we gotta make this quick."

"Yes, of course."

When Faivre parked and got out of her car, we greeted each other with an unusually prolonged embrace. "What's up?" I asked as we power-walked toward my office, reaching the building's entrance in record time.

"Oh, well, I mean nothing, really," she said, trying to catch her breath as I began racing up the stairs, skipping every other step. "Everything's fine, it all worked itself out, I just really wanted to see you," she said vaguely.

Why is everyone so socially awkward today? It's official: I work with a bunch of weirdos incapable of having a normal conversation. "Okay, well, if you change your mind and want to talk, you know where to find me."

I entered my office and beelined for my desk, toting posters and a gym bag, flashing my coworkers an enthusiastic smile. As I set my belongings down, it dawned on me that no one had greeted me, which was strange in our tight-knit working environment. The typical "Hey, doll," "Hey, you," or my personal favorite, "HAAAAZZZZ" (said in the most obnoxious voice one could imagine) had never come.

Looking up from my desk, I glanced to my right, where I saw my coworker and work mama Lisa slowly rocking back and forth in her chair. Her nose was beet red and her eyes were filled with tears screaming for permission to fall. I looked to my left and saw Master Chief pacing in his office doorway, gnawing on the knuckle of his pointer finger, his typical nervous tic. I stared at him as he walked from one side of his office doorway to the other. A pacing Master Chief is never a good sign. His back-and-forth shuffling coupled with the gnawing was beginning to make me exceptionally anxious.

"Good morning, Master Chief," I cheerfully said, purposefully interrupting him mid-pace.

He stopped, crossed his arms, and leaned against his door frame, staring me dead in the eyes for a few uncomfortable moments. His eyes looked as though they had so much to say, so much to apologize for. I stood in front of him, mirroring his crossed-arms pose, and waited for him to break his silence.

"Good morning, Haz" he said in a tone I didn't recognize. It was distant, shaky, and unsure. "Why don't you follow me into the CO's (commanding officer's) office."

"Yeah, sure. I mean, of course. Can you fill me in on what this is all about? Or what I've done wrong?" I pleaded. "It's been eating at me all morning."

Because we had such a close working relationship, I figured Master Chief Peirsel would extend the courtesy of cluing me in—or would at least give me the tiniest sliver of information—before I entered this unexpected meeting with the CO in charge of our entire base.

"It's going to be fine. You...you will be fine," he replied, motioning for me to start walking.

I followed him down the hallway, turning my head in

search of answers. Faivre had returned and was standing at my desk with Lisa alongside her. I shot them both an obviously perplexed look, one that screamed, "What the fuck? Help me out, people!" I needed at least one of them to mouth a clue, whisper a word of encouragement, or simply give me a look of reassurance. No such luck.

The twenty-foot walk to my Captain's office felt like a half-marathon, but we eventually made it. Master Chief and I stood shoulder-to-shoulder, staring at the shiny letters on the solid oak door in front of us. CAPTAIN PETE DAWSON. He took a brief breath before he leaned in to knock. As my heart pounded out of my chest, I couldn't think straight. I anxiously grabbed his elbow, which stopped his fist from making contact with the door. He pulled back and I began to whisper, "Master Chief, PLEASE, PLEASE just tell me something. Anything. I don't want to go in there looking like an idiot, having zero clue what I'm walking into!"

"Haz, it's going to be okay," he said again, knocking before I could stop him a second time.

"Come in."

I followed Master Chief's lead as he opened the door and walked inside. Once in the office, I stood at attention in front of my CO while Master Chief Peirsel shut the door and took his place behind me.

"Good morning, sir," I said with a smile.

"Morning, Petty Officer. Please take a seat."

A junior sailor is rarely seen casually sitting in a chair in front of their CO, so I made sure to glance back at Master Chief for a nod of approval. He gave me a quick one and I complied. My ass had not yet hit the vinyl when my CO casually blurted out three devastating words.

"Sean is dead."

Falling into the chair, I parroted: "Sean is dead. What do you mean, 'Sean is dead?' NO NO NO. PLEASE, GOD, NO."

"He died last night, around 0030 (12:30 a.m.) local time. Afghanistan called at 0530 this morning to confirm the loss."

"How? How did he die?"

"He was shot and succumbed to his injury."

"No! No...!" I must have screamed that a dozen times. Master Chief wrapped his arms around me, our tears quiet as pin drops, falling to the floor. Collectively, they created a small puddle that encompassed our agony.

Right there, twenty feet away from the desk I had sat at for the last two years, I made the painful transition from wife to widow. There was no white sedan creeping up to my house, no chaplain to properly deliver the news, no casualty officer behind him ready with answers to the assortment of questions I'd ask. No one was there who should've been to properly navigate me through the fiery hell I was forced to walk through that day. Tears came crashing down as I pleaded for my husband to come back to me. My smart-as-hell-but-extremely-socially-awkward Captain sat and stared, never once offering his condolences. No tears fell from his face, which betrayed no hint of the suffering every soul in that room was experiencing. He just sat there, silent, a quiet observer of the tangible agony that consumed me.

So there I was, in my place of work, dressed in uniform, crying in front of my commanding officer. I was caught in the crosshairs of maintaining some sort of military bearing, while simultaneously being a human currently suffering the greatest of losses.

"I need to get out of here. Can I please just get out of here? Are we done here? Can we just be done here?"

"Head into my office. There are some things Captain Dawson and I need to figure out, so it's all yours for the time being," Master Chief painfully whispered. Captain Dawson nodded his approval.

As I beelined for his office, fighting back tears of anguish, I saw the people who had let me down that day in the distance. The chaplain was dressed in his crisp dress white uniform, champing at the bit to offer his condolences, and the command assistance casualty officer (CACO) was feverishly filling out paperwork.

There's a specific military protocol for when a sailor passes away. The government-issued sedan, the chaplain in dress uniform standing shoulder-to-shoulder with the CACO; you see these, and you brace for impact. You know the completely whole person who answers that door will be reduced to small remnants by the time she turns around to shut it. The responsibility for that painstaking transition, from whole to broken, lies on the shoulders of the people who have been trained to handle this devastating duty. They'd been expected to answer the call of duty at 0530 (5:30 a.m.) that morning, and they'd failed to act. Now, the base's public affairs officer was knocking on the CMC's door every thirty minutes trying to get a statement from me to release to the public. It was all too much. Before I'd even stepped foot in the office that morning, the Captain's plan, more or less, had been to hold me hostage at work until he figured out what to do.

Later, I learned that Favs was called in the wee hours of the morning by a sailor on duty who had just taken a call from Afghanistan reporting that one of our K9 handlers had been killed in the line of duty. The sailor needed the number of who to call next, and Favs knew the name and number of everyone important. She also knew Sean was the only K9 handler deployed from our base, and confirmed it was him prior to hanging up. That is why she requested I wait for her before going into work that morning, so she could be near when I was given the news.

Master Chief Peirsel found out shortly thereafter, and began calling in all personnel necessary to gain more information from the desert. He also briefed Captain Dawson on Sean's marital status, pointing out that as his wife, I was his next of kin. Captain Dawson had made it crystal clear that he would be the one to deliver the news to me and that the CACO and chaplain should be briefed, but should hide in a room downstairs so I wouldn't "know" what was happening. Everyone knew that morning, from as high-ranking as the Captain to as low as Favs—except for me. I made phone calls, ran errands, and waited for friends, while everyone around me was preparing for my arrival, constructing my big "surprise."

Sean and I were both in the military, which is not unusual. Many married couples serve. It is uncommon, however, for one spouse to be killed in action while the other is also on active duty. This unique situation had left my command confused about what to do. They didn't know whether to notify me at my house, or notify me when I reported to work; whether to let me go home and grieve, or keep me in an office under supervision; whether to treat me as a sailor, or as a widow.

Sean's death had drawn a line in the sand. On one side was the oath I'd taken to serve and protect, and the contract that bound me there. On the other was a newly widowed woman who needed time to grieve. While leadership hashed out which side of the line they fell on and what that meant, I called my parents in Arizona and told them the news. As the sun set, they touched down in Washington, and I was finally granted permission to go home.

DRESS BLUES

My first night at home, I felt like someone was holding me underwater. It was hard to breathe, to eat, to move. Fear paralyzed me and prevented me from kicking up to the surface: fear about what a life without Sean might look like. Fear that he'd died in pain. Fear that he'd died alone. Fear that I'd never really know. The ocean was my grief and it was killing me.

I took to sleeping under the dining room table with a sheet draped over it, so I couldn't see the apartment that Sean and I had called home. My mom eventually crawled under the table with me, rubbing my back as

I cried, speechless over the tragedy that had just taken place. My dad flip-flopped between sitting on the couch, asking what he could do, and pacing my two-bedroom condo. For the first time in either of our lives, there was something he couldn't help me fix, as there would be no putting Sean back together. I recall that night like snapshots: still images from the times I managed to pry my swollen eyes open, only to remember where I was and start crying again, blurring my vision...and then, blackness.

I awoke the day after Sean's death to my mom's voice gently calling my name. "Allie." I pretended not to hear her, figuring if I didn't open my eyes and didn't leave my place under the table, then I wouldn't have to face the reality that Sean was dead and so was our future. "Al, you've got to get up, babe. We need to get you packed and ready for the airport." I opened my swollen, bloodshot eyes, lifted a tiny corner of the sheet, and gave my mom a solemn nod of acknowledgment.

Lifting the pearly white sheet and dragging my lifeless body out from under the table felt like an enormous feat. My insides were raw and my body felt heavy. The knowledge that we were headed to Dover Air Force Base, the place where the heroes who have perished come home, to receive Sean's remains hung like a weight on my every move. Every step down the hallway to the room Sean and

I had shared felt forced. Tears streamed down my face as I began to rummage through our dresser. Eventually, my mom entered the room and realized that packing was a larger task than I could bear. "Why don't you go sit with your dad on the couch, Al? I can take it from here."

I sat on our bed instead, clinging to Sean's dress blue uniform top, sobbing into the area where his chest would have been, acting as though he was wearing it. Desperately grasping onto what I had left of Sean, I rocked myself back and forth, pinching myself and thinking, This has to be some sort of sick joke.

It wasn't.

On May 31, my sisters-in-arms Jessica and Mona knocked on the door and greeted me with hugs and condolences. By now I had Sean's uniform top draped over my body, the dark blue arms draped around my neck like Sean was hugging me. "We need to get you guys to the airport, sister. Are you ready to go?" I wasn't. I wasn't ready to face a world without Sean—a world where people were moving on, while I was stuck. My parents gave them a quick nod of approval as we all shuffled out the door, suitcases in tow. Outside, the Seattle sky was dark and rainy, and for once I was happy the sun wasn't shining. It was fitting.

As we headed toward the airport, we picked up my Master

Chief, whose swollen eyes were evidence of the fact he wasn't faring much better than me. He took his seat near the front of the van and let out a quiet, "Morning, everyone." He turned and glanced at me and I quickly turned my head. I hadn't spoken much since Sean's death and I had no intention of starting then.

"Has she had his uniform like that all morning?" he whispered to my parents.

"Yes, and she won't set it down," my mom told him.

"Let me know what you need, Haz."

I nodded at him and continued to sob.

At the airport, a kind USO agent escorted us through security and boarded the plane with us to make sure we got seats together. She informed the flight crew of our circumstances. I was distantly grateful for her service, but anxious about seeing Sean's family when we landed. I knew seeing them and feeling the grief we all shared would make Sean's death real. A part of me was still in denial, still trapped in this place where Sean was on deployment and our future was still bright.

Luckily, upon arrival, Sean's sister Kelly ran to me first. We'd always been close, and I recognized her disbelief as my own. She roomed with me at The Fisher House, a beautiful, retreat-like space where we'd stay for several days while we planned Sean's memorial and interment services in Arlington. There were marble floors, endless snacks, and a staff to get us anything we needed. Anything, that is, except for Sean. I spent most of that time in bed, refusing to eat the food that Master Chief kept setting outside my door. "Haz, you gotta eat" he'd say. His requests went ignored. There were plans and decisions to be made, decisions that we couldn't hold off on any longer.

I heard a knock at the door and saw Kelly pop her head in. She walked in, quietly shutting the door behind her, and crawled into bed with me. Rubbing my back, she began to speak, "Sis, I know how hard this is. It's so hard."

"I can't do it, Kel. I can't go out there and plan my husband's funeral. I can't do it. We had so many hopes and dreams and plans for the future and now this is all I have left." I gripped his dress blues tighter.

"Sean's not in that top, Al. He's in everything we see and touch and experience. He's in your heart. He's with us, and he always will be."

Heartened by her words, for the first time in days I undraped Sean's uniform from my body, and left it on the bed where we'd been lying. I had a ceremony to plan, and a husband to make proud.

DANCE OF GRIEF

Like perfectionism, grief in many ways is never-ending. It's not something you ever really get over. I therefore relied on my perfectionist tendencies, which felt so natural and comfortable during this time, to get me through Sean's death. If I'm going to be a widow, I thought, I'm going to be the perfect widow. I will honor my husband and keep his memory and legacy alive.

As much as I was determined to hold myself together, I was sent spiraling en route to meet Sean's body. We—our family, my Command Master Chief, several colleagues, and myself—all boarded a bus to the tarmac, and I started crying hysterically. Plane-side, I waited for everyone else to get off so I could sit on the bus and pull myself together. Just when I thought I was alone, I felt a hand on my shoulder. I looked up to see my old commanding officer, a great man and one of my biggest mentors, Captain Olsen, standing before me. "Oh, my God," I said. "You're here!"

"Haz," he greeted me, choosing his words carefully. "I need you to pull it together. For Sean, for his family, for his friends, for your own sake. You need to be strong. You've got this." He said it softly, and I'm not sure whether he knew how much power his suggestion carried. I pulled it together immediately. I stopped crying and clambered off the bus, taking my place in line beside the rest of my family, the K9 handlers, and their dogs.

As men in uniform carried Sean's flag-draped casket off the plane and into the waiting hearse, I wanted so badly to walk over and touch the top of the box where my husband's body lay. I wanted to wrap my arms around it and tell him everything I'd been wanting to say since the moment he'd died, but I didn't. I couldn't. On the tarmac, there was a line and a rope that prevented you from going beyond that marked distance. So I merely watched, mute, as my husband—now considered government property, at least until a full autopsy could be performed—went by. The K9s started howling like they knew they had lost one of their own. It was so beautiful to hear so many K9s howl at the mere presence of Sean's casket. In that moment, I knew Sean was smiling from the heavens, watching us welcome such a beautifully brave hero home.

I don't remember much else from the weeks leading up to Sean's funeral. Friends dropped in and out to comfort me and share memories. The base held a memorial service for Sean, where we all grieved and paid tribute to a heroic man whose life had ended way too soon. I cried more tears than ever before behind closed doors, but stood tall and stayed strong in public. I wanted to appear put-together and strong—strong for Sean, strong for us.

As a result, I didn't process my emotions in a healthy, natural way. I stopped grieving when I forced myself to stop feeling my grief. I kept focusing on doing the next thing: checking in on Sean's kennel master and fellow K9 handlers, seeing to Sean's dog Sicario when he came home, calling all of my and Sean's friends periodically to ensure they were doing okay. But I wouldn't let anyone do the same for me.

I saw grief as either/or, black or white. Either you're a graceful, pulled-together widow, or an overly emotional mess. I could either be loyal to Sean's legacy, blogging and posting about him, and going to visit Arlington every other month, or I could check out and wallow in grief. I didn't want to ever forget Sean and the joy and love he'd brought to my life. I also didn't know how I'd ever love again without somehow feeling like an adulteress—so deep was my love for Sean.

What I realized, years down the road, is that grief is a dance. It's not black or white, but somewhere in-between, a dance between the lanes. One day you wallow; the next, you tentatively laugh at a friend's joke. Some days you're a little bit sad, but still happy. It goes in waves like that. On your best days, you can almost remember what it was like to be on the beach, sun shining, building your fairytale castle with the love of your life. On your worst, you're back in the deep end, choking.

What this means is that you can be madly in love with what you lost at the same time that you can be madly in love with the present. When you embrace both, it's like taking a super deep breath and feeling the air in your body buoy you to the surface. It doesn't mean you no longer care about the love you lost, but it does mean you're beginning to move forward, an arm's length closer to shore. That's the direction I hoped I was heading, anyway, even if Sean was no longer there waiting with open arms.

ON SETBACKS

Just as I was establishing my new normal and finally figuring out how to navigate life as a sailor, a mother, and a widow, my contract with the military expired. I had to decide whether to re-commit or get out. Since enlisting, I'd always planned to make a career of the Navy. I liked the work and I was good at it—plus, it kept me as close as possible to the memory of my beloved. At the same time, though, I'd begun to suffer symptoms of PTSD from Senior Chief's multiple assaults.

If I were to deploy to Afghanistan (it was a dream of mine to visit the place where Sean had last been alive), there was no telling how my body and mind might handle the experience. Fortunately or unfortunately, depending on how you look at it, the decision ended up not being mine to make.

In the months following Sean's death, I'd begun seeing a military counselor, and then a military psychiatrist, for general anxiety. It was affecting my performance at work. Some things—generally, male leadership—would trigger a flashback of my abuse at the hands of my Senior Chief, and I'd have a panic attack. The only way for me to calm down was to take a brown paper bag into a dark closet and breathe slowly and deliberately until my racing pulse subsided. Of course, male leadership is pretty dang hard to avoid in the Navy.

These episodes went on my medical record, along with the hysterectomy I'd undergone after the botched delivery at the Naval hospital. Before I could re-enlist, my medical records were sent to the Navy's medical board for review. The board would determine if I was fit for full duty, or would have to be medically separated from the service. All I could do was wait.

Two months later, the medical board sent my command its findings. When I got the news, I headed straight to the admin office to review them. Staring at the warm paper, fresh off the printer, I read the words "Medically retired." After four long years, my service to the country I cherished and loved was done. Within weeks I'd move out of the condo Sean and I shared and into a house in Arizona.

As much I'd wanted to get to Afghanistan, I knew that

being in that hell hole wouldn't bring me the closure I so desperately yearned for. So I accepted my fate, feeling good about the fact that the Navy had acknowledged that they'd fucked me. A monthly check of restitution didn't take away all that had occurred during my time in the service, but it felt good to be seen, heard, and believed. That was something I could hang my hat on.

My day of separation finally came and went. When I moved back to Arizona, I took Sean's memory with me, and settled down in the house I had bought for Addisen and myself merely four weeks prior. I wanted to set some roots right away for Addisen's sake. I wanted to gain some stability after our world had been torn apart. At three, she adjusted well. The transition was much harder for me. I'd truly found myself in the military and had thrived within its structured environment. Suddenly, no one was telling me where to be and when, what to wear and how to wear it, how to do my hair and how not to.

I felt lost. Basic things stymied me: I didn't even know how to fill a prescription at a civilian pharmacy for fuck's sake. On top of all that, I was still grieving hard. Sean and I had just started a whole new life together and planned a well-thought-out future. He'd made me the happiest I'd ever been. Without him, I was the emptiest I'd ever been. Forget about trying to clear the bar. My bar had been knocked clean away. I no longer knew what to aim for, or what direction my life was headed in.

BULLETPROOF

To force a sort of pseudo-structure on my life, I immediately joined a gym and got a new personal trainer. I found an awesome preschool for Addisen and would drop her off every morning, then head to the gym where I'd meet with my trainer for an hour. Afterward, I'd do another hour of cardio on my own, head home for a quick lunch, then go and run miles around the canal near my house. It wasn't the same canal I'd once run with my best friend Bridget, but the idea was the same. When it was time to pick Addisen up from school, I'd put her in the stroller and run around the block with her. After she went to bed at night, I'd top off my day with Insanity, a total body fitness program I had on DVD.

I was working out four or five hours a day, which was its own kind of insanity. But during those four or five hours, my thoughts dissipated—I focused only on the workout at hand. That was the whole goal: don't think, just do. The more I threw myself into exercise, the less time I had to worry, or ruminate, or feel. Very quickly, it became a compulsion, a throwback to my old obsession with perfectionism. If everything in my life is going to be this imperfect, this out of control, I thought, then I'm going to make myself bulletproof. I thought if I could armor my outside appearance with long, lean muscles, making it look like I had complete control over my life, then it would in turn mask the pain and emotions that were swirling around on the inside. I was consumed by this goal. The only exceptions to my extreme regimen were making plenty of time for Addie—she was and continues to be my whole world—and school. Having finally tapped into my GI bill, I was taking college courses online and blocking out time to work on them after Addie went to bed.

Despite living super close to my parents again, and many of my old friends from high school, I consciously cut off most human connection. Between my daily marathon workout sessions and playing student and single mother, I just didn't have any time. Or rather, depressed and withdrawn, I made sure I didn't have any time. My parents noticed my reclusiveness, but didn't know what to do about it. Bridget continued to stand by me. She was just about the only person in my world I made time for.

The only place I really made my presence known was online. I started blogging about Sean's and my experiences in the military in the form of long, overly detailed Facebook posts. The responses I got were encouraging. People posted comments to the effect of "Oh, my God! I shared your post so other people can know the reality of servicemen and women getting killed in Afghanistan," or "I'm sharing your post because it's so beautifully written," or "I'm here for you if you need anything." Blogging and posting about my experience gave me the platform I needed to work through my feelings. Each entry I typed was a reprieve from the isolation I had built for myself.

Although most people offered words of support and love, some would message me and express their concerns about me not moving on, telling me, "It's okay to let go," as if the death of my husband was some mundane event that I should've gotten over a year ago (eye roll). I also received messages of concern over how thin I had gotten, how sad I looked in a photo, and my all-time favorite, how "consumed" I still seemed to be by the death of Sean.

Opinions, opinions, opinions! Everyone has one, and if you take all of them on board, you're bound to sink. I quickly adopted a system to navigate through all the shit people felt so utterly entitled to say. Unless you are in the depths, treading water and weathering the waves, then your opinion of how I choose to walk through storms is null and void. I give no weight to the opinions of people who are viewing my struggles from the safety of the shore. They are just as irrelevant as they are cheap.

For eight months, I only took phone calls from those who'd proven themselves to be in my court, like Bridget and Amy Abbott. We'd talk on the phone for hours, late at night, coffee in hand. They fearlessly got in the water with me, and as we bore the waves together, they would listen intently, and offer feedback and support. They and a few others formed my Circle of Trust, and every one of them remains in it to this day. That's important: to know that you can ignore the haters, the opinions from the cheap seats, but you don't have to go it alone. In fact, when it comes to overcoming setbacks, support is vital!

About a year and a half after Sean's death, Sean's best friend, Christopher Roybal, came to visit me. Although he lived one state away in California, he was part of my Circle because he called almost daily to talk. When I answered the door, Christopher was taken aback. "Jesus, Allie," he yelled out in surprise, "you need to eat a cheeseburger and drink a fucking chocolate shake, you look like a skeleton." For the first time, I allowed myself to truly hear someone out when it came to my lifeline, exercise. I'd been writing everyone else's warnings off because, as I saw it, exercise was a much healthier alternative to the other ways people sometimes cope with grief. Chris helped me to see it was not. He challenged me to keep a log of my workouts, so that I'd have to confront their frequency. On the weekends, I realized, I'd been taking four-year-old Addisen to the track with me and having her stand on my weighted sled while I pulled it from one goal post to the other, her belly laugh trailing behind us. I did it "for fun." It wasn't fun; it was insane. I was missing out on life.

I realized then that since Sean's death, I'd been like an Instant Pot pressure-cooking away on high at all times. Exercising was the only way I knew to release the steam and feel better. I had so much grief bottled up inside me, but I wasn't handling it in a way that served me or my daughter. I vowed to cut back and create space for activities and life, outside of working out.

Then I got sick.

THE HOLE

Mid-2013, I started feeling nauseous all the time. I would throw up over and over again until I was throwing up blood on a near-daily basis. Those who knew me said it was overexertion: "You're just working out too much."

"No," I insisted, fighting back, "it doesn't feel like that. I'm replacing my electrolytes, and I've cut way back."

Finally, I went to see my doctor. He ran copious tests and determined that my body was making excess calcium. He sent me to an endocrinologist who ultimately diagnosed me with a condition of the parathyroid gland—the gland that produces parathyroid hormone, which in turn regulates the blood's calcium level. I was producing too much hormone; therefore, too much calcium.

After several months, my hormones normalized somewhat and I quit throwing up blood.

I wish I could say that it ended there—that I got my exercise addiction under control, and my calcium levels regulated; that Sean's loss quit hurting so much; that the rawness and pain of all the trauma I had endured ceased to exist. The truth is that I was back in that log flume, climbing inch by inch up a steep incline, and while it seemed like life was trending in the right direction—onwards and upwards—in reality I was getting ready for the drop. I just couldn't see it yet. I didn't know how far down I could fall, or that the chute would jump and dip erratically thereafter for an indefinite amount of time. All I knew was that one day I had been healthy and working toward happiness, and the next I was throwing up and so tired I couldn't get out of bed. I needed a way to deal with these setbacks that would nurture me, and give me the time and space to heal. So I created one.

I call it The Hole—and I literally picture it like a hole in the ground. To me, The Hole is the thing you step in that makes you stumble when you're otherwise out for a relaxing, late summer walk. It's every setback, every roadblock, every unsolicited opinion that upends your day or your plans or your mood, and sprains your metaphorical ankle. In other words, it's not a life-ending complication, but it definitely rains on your parade. It's okay to stumble and get stuck in The Hole—it's impossible to avoid 100 percent of the time—but you can't just stay there forever. I always give myself a day: a full twenty-four hours to feel sorry for myself and take care of myself in whatever way needed. Then I get up, dust myself off, leave all the drama and fuckery behind, and climb out, trudging forward and pushing past whatever pain led me there.

I started using this trick around the time of the court-martial. Today I find it more comforting than ever. For one day, I stop measuring myself against the invisible bar. For one day I grieve, making my peace with whatever pain point needs addressed, no other expectations. It's like ceasing to struggle against the riptide and trusting, for once, the dead-man's float. Like saying, "Sit with me, pain, and teach me everything I need to know before I move forward."

I take that rest, that reprieve, that time in The Hole, and you can too. So that when the time comes, you can keep treading, and if life calls for it, start the long swim back to shore. It's uncomfortable, this sitting, this resting in The Hole, because The Hole is full of shit, pain, anger, and a plethora of other unsettling emotions. But I challenge you to sit and lean into the discomfort. Emotions are teachers. Let them do what they came here to do.

ON RESILIENCY

After my diagnosis, I scaled back my extreme workout regime and learned a healthier appreciation for the limits of my body. Still, I wasn't completely healed. My calcium levels remained unstable, fluctuating between hypercalcemia and hypocalcemia, meaning at times my body wasn't producing enough calcium. It manifested first as numbness in my hands and feet. They'd get all tingly and not work right; it was difficult to walk. Then my heart started skipping beats. The worst symptom, however, was involuntary muscle contraction. It looked like I was having seizures, though in reality, I just couldn't stop my muscles from convulsing uncontrollably.

One day when I was a particularly hot mess, my good friend and roommate at the time took me to the hospital while another friend watched Addie. My doctor determined that my oxygen levels were dangerously low and my body needed uninterrupted time to replenish my calcium. Right then and there, she placed me in a medically induced coma.

I have no idea what happened while I was under. When I awoke, I looked around the strange hospital room, which seemed *way* too brightly lit, and attempted to blink back the rising tide of panic. *How long have I been out? Where's my daughter? Is that my mom over there?* Mom had a horrified look on her face, like she was staring at a dead person. *Am I dead? Why is it so bright in here?* Next to her, I thought I recognized one of my closest confidants. She seemed blurry and hard to make out, but her smile was easy to recognize. To make sure, I opened my eyes as wide as they would go— fighting the heavy medication I was under. With mounting urgency and every ounce of energy I could muster, I forced them open. *Yes, that's Mom. Yes, there's Katie.* I began fighting the breathing tube that was lodged in my airway and attempted to speak. I failed. Katie ran to the nurses' station and came back bearing a white board and a marker. As fast as I could, I wrote my urgent question: "Where's Addisen?"

"She's safe, babe," my mom reassured me. "She's at your house. Bekah and Brit are watching her. It's okay." She rubbed a few sweaty strands of hair from my forehead.

The nursing staff made me fight my breathing tube for

an additional thirty excruciating minutes until they were sure I could breathe on my own. Then they removed it.

Perhaps it was a combination of the meds, my confusion, and a brief but real moment of certainty that I was dead, but the next thing I knew, I was bawling. I felt completely overcome with grief in a way I hadn't experienced since Sean's death. I felt as though I was mourning another death: my own—or rather, the version of me that I had always known. I guess I naively thought that everything would somehow return to normal after my diagnosis, that eventually I'd be fine. But I wasn't, and on the brink of consciousness between sleeping and waking, I finally realized I never would be fine again. I'd spend the rest of my life in and out of the hospital, unable to predict when and where another hypocalcemic episode would send me back for another calcium infusion. "Sick" was to be my new normal. As I wept, I let go of what had been and struggled to accept what was. *This is me now. This is my life.* I wasn't able to make my peace with that fact that very day, but it kickstarted the process of feeling out my new boundaries and embracing, in spite of it all, my own resiliency.

TAKING ON THE WORLD TOGETHER

Before the medically induced coma, I'd decided to follow my lifelong dream and enroll in nursing school. It was near the end of 2014, and I was determined to move on despite my health issues. Because Arizona schools still had three-year waitlists, I'd applied and been accepted to Morningside College in my birth state of Iowa. In January 2015, I packed up Addie and our house and moved us out to Sioux City, where she and I would take on the world together. The day she started kindergarten, I started my freshman year, and it felt like life was looking up.

I got sick again that spring. After coming out of the coma, I returned to classes against my family's wishes. They thought the stress of school and single parenting was too much for someone with a chronic disease, but parts of the old me were still very much alive and well, still hellbent on proving to myself and others that I could do something incredible with my life, that my illness did not define me. This meant my parents had to fly back and forth to Iowa every time my calcium bottomed out and I had to endure yet another three- to five-day hospital stay. Sometimes, friends or classmates in Sioux City would rally and watch Addisen until my parents could get there, which inconvenienced everyone, even if they never said as much.

The summer after my sophomore year, Addie and I went home to Arizona for a visit. Floating in my parents' pool one afternoon, I realized how much I'd been asking of everyone around me. The flights, the time off, and the stress they'd endured through all of it could no longer be justified. I couldn't just quit, though, could I? This time, I could. Even though I was able to make great grades, even though I was able to juggle being a single mother while I did it, even though I'd proven to myself that I could do hard and scary things, it simply wasn't fair. I'd promised myself there'd be no turning back, but I'd also promised Addie a happy, stable life. I was coming to realize that I wasn't giving her what I'd intended, and I was making life miserable for everyone else.

From my pool floatie, I announced that for the sake of Addisen and my family, I would not be returning to nursing school. I felt defeated as the words slipped from my mouth. It was as if I'd been launched back into the depths after working so hard to reach the shore, with no lifeboat in sight. Struggling to keep my head above water, I held my breath and waited. Waited for a disappointed reaction, waited for encouragement to keep trying, waited for a huge wave to come crashing over me and swallow me whole.

"Allie, we are so proud of you and all the hard work you've put into this chapter of your life. But due to your health, Dad and I couldn't agree more," Mom said with vigor and enthusiasm.

I was relieved. It was as if the roaring waves and rumbles from the sky had dissipated, and only dark, rain-filled clouds remained. They were proud, which put me at ease, but I couldn't help but feel a small ripple of disappointment, too. I hadn't finished what I'd headed out to Iowa to do: get my degree and prove to myself that despite all the things that had set me back, I could start and finish something as important as my education. Furthermore, I wanted to show Addie that it didn't matter what obstacles might come her way in life—she could do the same thing.

Dreams dashed, my RN fantasies dissolved right there in the water. I stopped planning for my future, because the future was too unknown. I no longer had a say-so, I believed, in how my life was going to go. As with Sean's death and Senior Chief sexually assaulting me, things happened *to* me—not *for* me, or because I'd worked for them. I hadn't asked for my husband to die. I hadn't asked to be abused. I certainly hadn't asked to get sick. Fate was picking on me.

I climbed into The Hole and I bent my own rule, staying there far longer than the usual twenty-four hours. I cried and mourned and kicked and screamed over everything I'd thought my life would be, until it was time to get back up. Admittedly, staying in The Hole forever felt more appealing than getting out. Pulling out my white flag, surrendering, giving up, felt safer than facing another day on the merry-go-round I seemed to be on. Although tempting, I refused to give up. It may end the temporary problems of our todays, but like a thief in the night, giving up ends the opportunities of our tomorrows, too. So, step by step, one foot after the other, I managed to fight my way forward, leaving my white flag in the dust.

Today I often think about my extended period in The Hole and realize what a waste it would have been to just give up, curl up, and quit. All of the incredible things that have happened and continue to happen in my life were and are not born from fictitious sandcastles on the sandy beach—they were and are born from the fire. As horrific and pain-filled as it is to walk through the flames, the amount of life that lies directly on the other side always makes the suffering worth it.

If you decide to climb out of The Hole and join me in the blaze, and I hope you do, don't fret over the scars that remain when the embers reduce to ash. They will remind you of where you've been, the hell you've walked through, and how much life and perspective you've gained by doing so. They will fuel you and vigorously push you forward the next time you're torn between surrendering to your current circumstance or continuing forward in spite of it.

As you move forward in your journey, I hope you remember that scars are reserved for the shit-trudging, hole-climbing, water-treading, fire-walking FIGHTERS—

and every single person on this planet, including you, has the ability to be one!

LOVE CONQUERS ALL

My choice to leave nursing school was the first of two major decisions I had to make that year. The second was for love.

Just before Addie and I moved to Iowa, I'd reconnected with my seventh-grade boyfriend, Dodger. His family and I had stayed in touch since middle school, but it was the first time he and I had talked in many years. I reached out one day to suggest we meet up for dinner and a catch-up sesh, and the rest was history. I made it a priority to visit home as often as possible, and with Bridget in tow, Dodger would visit Iowa. We weren't dating exactly, because we weren't sleeping together, but we weren't seeing other people, either. I called it "exclusively talking," which equated to: "I really like you, I can't see myself with anyone else, but I'm scared as shit. So let's not put a title on this."

By the time I made my way back to Arizona, the whole no-title thing had worked for a year. But the whole scared-to-death, one-foot-in, one-foot-out ordeal ended suddenly when Dodger gave me an ultimatum, similar to the one I'd once given Sean. "I love you to death, Allie,"

Dodger said, "but I can't continue half-in and half-out like this. I want all of you. I deserve that. And if you can't give me that, I don't think I can do this anymore."

I didn't know what to say at first. I was terrified that as soon I let Dodger in, he would die, or leave. I was also scared that by saying yes to him, I would be signing him up for a life of suffering, too. For his part, Dodger had tried everything he could to assuage those fears. He'd visited me all the time in the hospital, setting Addie between him and me, so we could play board games or color in bed. He'd listened compassionately as I'd talked about Sean and how heavily his presence is still felt. He'd offered support as I'd attempted to walk through the assaults. He'd brightened every rough patch, helping me to turn tragedies into triumphs. Dodger promised me that no matter what I decided, he'd still be my friend, still be there for Addisen and me—but he needed an answer. Knowing he deserved one, I didn't take long to deliver it.

"You're right: you deserve better than a fear-stricken woman, terrified of what might happen if she lets you in. But I will never know what happens unless I let you in, all the way in, so let's do this," I cheerfully said.

I thought back to middle school, to the first time we'd dated. We'd stayed together the whole seventh-grade school year, significant for a couple of twelve-year-olds.

The summer before eighth grade, he'd found a new group of friends—"super popular" ones—and they'd told him to break up with me, which he'd promptly done over the phone. I remember calling him right back and saying, "It's fine if you're breaking up with me, but it's more respectful to do so in person and I wish you would have done that." He'd agreed and apologized. With that kind of honesty and clear communication flavoring our earliest interactions, it didn't surprise me that he'd stuck by my side through what proved to be some of my lowest points in the hospital. He'd seen me convulse, go numb, and act irritable, and he hadn't turned around and run. Popularity no longer mattered a whit, because what we had and have is real. Life had been tough, but he made it more bearable. He offered me a hand up out of The Hole.

Deciding to let Dodger in fully was, in the end, a no-brainer. I've never stopped worrying that I will lose him, but I've accepted that I don't know when that will be. He could die on the way to work tomorrow, or when we're ninety. All I know is life with Dodger always has and always will trump life without Dodger.

March 22, 2017, my birthday, Dodger got down on one knee amongst our closest family and friends, and proposed. November 17, 2017, a mere eight months later, we became husband and wife.

A NEW DAY

Eventually, a drug called Natpara soared through all of its clinical trials and became available to patients like me. Natpara is a daily injection of synthetic parathyroid hormone that stabilizes my erratic calcium levels. It's not a perfect drug, it doesn't stabilize my levels 100 percent of the time, but it has allowed me to build a life outside of comas and ICU visits. And that's something I believed was unachievable during my time treading water in the depths.

With Dodger and Addisen at my side, I feel like I've finally reached the shore again. It's been a long, exhausting struggle against the riptide, but it makes me appreciate the solid comfort of the warm sand between my toes and beneath my feet. I'm no longer constantly on the brink of drowning. I'm safe. Is every day a glistening, fun-filled day at the beach? Of course not! But, man, when you turn around and catch the first rays breaking through the darkness and making their appearance over the horizon, it finally signals the start of a new day, a better day, a day that you not only survive, but which sees you thrive.

If you're still in the depths, treading water and fighting the current, know that the light you've been waiting on is slowly making its way through the darkness. Know that at the other end of your suffering, the start of a new day, a better day, a day where you thrive, is waiting for you, too.

10

ON TRANSPARENCY

One dark fall night, Dodger and I tried out a new sex position. It wasn't anything like *Fifty Shades of Grey*, or really anything all that exciting. But it was new, at least to us. The first second or two I did okay, but as we continued, I had a flashback to Senior Chief assaulting me in the same position—except this time, I wasn't clothed, I was naked. I could no longer see my fiancé for who he was. When I looked at him, I truly and honestly mistook him for Senior Chief.

Oh my God, my irrational mind panicked. *Run, Allie, fucking run.* Before I knew it, Dodger was off me and in the bathroom. I grabbed my phone and quietly slipped out the back door and through our back gate onto the adjoining golf course. As soon as my bare feet hit the plush green grass, I began to sprint as fast as my little legs would go, disappearing into the darkness of the unlit course.

Picture this: It's nighttime. Middle of fall. I'm a twenty-eight-year-old woman sprinting down the fairway in bare feet. Frantically calling her mom. "He's after me," I scream when she answers. "Help me. Help me!"

"Who's after you, Allie?"

"Senior Chief. He's chasing me. He's going to hurt me. Please. Please!"

"Allie, no one's going to hurt you. It's okay. You're scaring me."

"Mom, I'm scared. I need you to come help me." (At this time, my parents lived less than ten minutes away.)

"Your dad is on his way. Where are you? Go to a street so he can find you."

I dovetail off the golf course and toward the nearest road, but keep my mom on the line. "I can't wait," I tell her, my tangible fear swallowing me whole. "Senior Chief's going to find me and get me."

Hanging up, I cross the street and jump the neighbors' fence. I don't know them, but hiding behind a bush in their backyard seems like a good idea. Mom calls me back a few minutes later. I scream at her to help me. The owner of the house steps out. He shines a light directly in my eyes. "Are you okay?"

I hang up on my mom again. "No, somebody's after me."

"Okay. It's okay. I'm not going to hurt you. You can come out."

"He's going to find me."

"We can go in the garage then. My kids are sleeping inside, but we can call the police from the garage and get you some help."

I'm reluctant. The man's wife steps outside. She quickly assesses the situation and helps to coax me out of the bush. I tiptoe through their house and enter their garage. They call the cops as promised. Then, using my phone, they call my mom to give her their address.

Unbeknownst to me, my parents call Dodger next and tell him where I am. He shows up at the neighbors' house shortly after they do. He opens the car door and immediately I'm protesting, "Keep him away from me, he's going to hurt me!"

"Who?" my mom asks.

"Him!" I point at Dodger.

"Allie, snap out of it!" Mom commands. "You're being crazy. That's Dodger. He would never hurt you."

Dodger stays an uncertain distance away until the cops arrive. One officer shines a blacklight on my fiancé's hands to see if his knuckles are bruised or if he has blood on them. All the while, my parents are explaining to the other cop, "She's a veteran. She has PTSD. She was medically retired for it. She might be having some sort of episode."

"All right," the officer says. "I'm not going to arrest anyone tonight, but these two have to separate."

Addisen's at a preplanned sleepover with friends so Dodger heads home to an empty house. I stay overnight with my parents. For the longest time, I can't fall asleep, positive that Senior Chief is coming for me, he knows where I am, he knows where my daughter is.

THAT WHICH CAN'T BE MEASURED

The next morning, I woke to bright sunlight playing across the walls of my parents' guest bedroom. Coherent and alert, I remembered the night before—how I'd acted; what I'd put everyone through, especially Dodger. I felt fucking terrible. I called and asked him to come over to my parents' house. "I'm so sorry," I said, repeating those three words over and over again, already bawling. "Please come. Please. I'm so incredibly sorry."

Dodger miraculously showed up. Meeting him at the doorway, I leapt into his arms and sobbed uncontrollably. After several minutes, I managed to pull myself together enough to explain what had been going through my mind less than twenty-four hours prior. "I thought you were Senior Chief, babe. Something about that position and demons from my past triggered something inside of me. You weren't you, our house wasn't our house, and I was back in the Navy. I was fighting, fighting for my life. I thought you were Senior Chief, I really did, and I am so sorry." I tried to explain the situation a million different ways, but none of them made any sort of sane sense. "I understand if you want to leave me after that. I completely get it; I'd leave me, too."

Without a moment of hesitation, Dodger blurted, "Absolutely not." I sighed in relief. "PTSD is a medical condition. While last night was scary, and maddening,

and shitty, I also understand that it was out of your con-
trol. I forgive you and I love you, and I sure as hell am
not leaving you."

From where I sat on my metaphorical shore, I promptly
threw up all the bilious saltwater that for years had been
sloshing around in my body. Not only had Dodger already
seen me "in sickness and in health," and dragged me to
shore despite my stubborn insistence that I do everything
myself, but now, I'd unintentionally almost sent him to
jail. While I knew I was safe—that Senior Chief was far, far
away—I was still dealing with the aftermath: the wreckage
after the tsunami; the fragile state of my own mind. My
entire life I had strived to be the perfect daughter, sister,
friend, and mother; but sitting there at my parents' house,
word-vomiting explanations and apologies to a kind and
understanding Dodger, it seemed the only kind of perfect
I had managed to become was perfectly broken. But kind
he was, and he combatted every single thing I said with
words of encouragement and affirmation. Never mind the
fact that I'd falsely accused him of harming me, or that
he could have gone to jail, or that I'd sent him home to
an empty house to try and piece together the chaos that
had just unfolded. Dodger loved me anyway. He loved
me for me and the past that comes with me. In his eyes, I
was perfect. Perfect for him. Golf course incident and all.

After that night, I immediately upped the number of

times per week I attended counseling. Unlike before, I became willing to do the hard work of diving deep, back into the ocean of my trauma, and talk about and process all it contained. As I did this, I was able to recognize that my past really had happened, but it wasn't *still* happening. I was safe on shore. Although it felt sometimes like the waves were pounding me, the choking sensation was all in my head. I'd (mostly) finished coughing up the seawater of my bottled emotions. I could relax on a soft beach towel under the sun and allow the mantle of perfection to slip from my aching shoulders.

When I did, I realized two things. First, if I wanted healthier relationships with Dodger, my parents, my friends, and myself, I'd have to become more transparent, dropping the facade of perfection. Strength, I came to understand, is not found in the phrase "I'm doing great" or in the pearly white smile that flawlessly masks pain and angst. No, the willingness to admit that things have fallen to shit and the ability to set your pride aside and reach for the hand trying to help you is where true strength is found. Feelings are not big, scary things that we need to keep hidden from the world. Feelings are normal, and sharing them opens you up for human affection.

The second thing I realized was the most important revelation of all: the bar of perfection, which had first manifested in my middle school psyche, *never existed*. I had created it, and I had continually moved it out of reach. There is no universal standard of perfection. To believe in one is to constantly undermine yourself, and compare yourself to that which can't be measured.

Prior to the golf course incident, I was living my life all "hashtag blessed," curating the image I wanted everyone to see. *Look at me, all thin and fit, rocking this whole single mom thing and killin' it in school.* No one knew what was going on inside of me. They couldn't. I'd been leading them on too convincingly. My first step, therefore, was to be radically transparent—like, point-blank, "Things are a fucking disaster, and I need your advice on what to do next."

One by one, I told my Circle of Trust what had happened on the golf course that night. It was amazingly hard to admit to what felt so shameful and wrong. "Yeah, this is what I did," I said to each in turn, "but I'm getting help now—a lot of it. I needed you to know where I'm currently at, and where I'm headed."

They were surprised—from the outside it had looked like everything was fine—but they also praised me for getting help, for having the courage to be vulnerable during this "dark night of the soul," and trusting that the sun would rise again. I was worried they wouldn't be so understanding, that my secret would betray me as weak, or out of control, or unlovable. Instead, each and every one of them showered me with validation, assuring me that admitting I needed help was strength in its purest form. They were *proud* of me: an emotion I'd believed for years had to be earned through perfection and impeccable performance. Not so.

I've come to realize that what I saw, and what most of society sees, as "flaws" are not flaws at all. They are simply the circumstances, abilities, feelings, and stories that make us who we are. Hiding behind the facade of Ultra-Fit-Body Betty, or Perfectly-Put-Together Patty, or Emotionless Emily to escape the reality of your truth or negative opinions from others is easy, and quite frankly, it's cheap. Anyone can do it, and most of us at one time or another have. Taking off the mask and being honest, forthcoming, and vulnerable is just as hard as it is scary; but being transparent and truthful also allows more love and admiration to flow into your life than any fake front ever could.

After transitioning from façade to frank, I now have a deeper understanding of and connection with my husband, daughter, family, and Circle—one that doesn't entail smoke and mirrors. Rather, it allows me, and *requires* me, to show up authentically. With time, I have learned to show myself forgiveness and acceptance, and to be vocal about where I've been and where I'm at. One vulnerable moment after another, I continue to tear down the stigma that says we have to have it 100 percent together 100 percent of the time. I have become okay with being "flawed" and "imperfect." In fact, I fully embrace it, and I implore you to do the same.

THE MAJOR CONUNDRUM OF MY LIFE

These days, Dodger and I are co-owners of a sober living company and drug and alcohol treatment center in Scottsdale. While I unfortunately don't get to interact with the clients as much as I'd like to (I'm basically the de facto interior designer for both companies), Dodger gets more one-on-one time with the clients as he coaches them and holds them accountable to their 12 Steps. I'm proud of the work we're doing there, and I enjoy working for a company that promotes transparency as one of its core values.

Although I've never personally struggled with substance abuse, I can relate to addiction recovery from the perspective of a former exercise-a-holic. If nothing else, I understand why a person might turn to something outside of themselves for help in coping with everything happening on the inside. Before I found counseling, my escape was running. I really believed it was saving me, when what I needed was saving from myself. Now, I work out five days a week, but for a much more reasonable amount of time than I did before—an hour, on average, per day—which fits the recommended guidelines for a woman of my age and ability. No matter what, I take two days off every week to rest and check in with myself, ensuring I'm not backsliding into old habits. I spend those days with my Circle and with Addisen, who at nine, is the guiding light of my life.

Addie's and my relationship has always been special; not just mother-daughter special, but special on a soul level—perhaps because she's been there all along. When I began to let people in more intentionally, I started with her, aware that everything she saw her mother say and do would to some degree impact the woman she becomes. For that reason, I've shown her that it's okay to cry, to be angry, to be not okay—that you don't have to be (falsely) happy-go-lucky all the time. I want her to see that emotions are real and they serve us; they don't need to be tamped down, ignored, or flat-out squelched through physical overexertion every day. She's seen how, once in a while, Mommy does have bad days. And when I do, I talk to her about it, ensuring that I include how I am choosing to respond to it. When things are imperfect, we practice a kind of perfect transparency, and suddenly the monster's not so scary. The insurmountable becomes more manageable and the riptide loses some of its pull.

I realized the profundity of this lesson when I was in a therapy session one sweltering hot Arizona day. I was describing to my counselor what felt like the major conundrum of my life: wanting to move forward, while still honoring my past. Being fully in love with what is, while loving what was. "How can I balance my very real, very deep love for Dodger, with my very real, very deep, very grief-filled love for Sean?" I asked her, tears streaming down my face. "How can I make sure I do that right?"

"Allie," she said, "There is no 'right' in this situation. It's not that black-or-white. There is no way to 'do' life, love, grief—any of it!—perfectly."

When I shrugged her off, she repeated her statement. The second time, it clicked in my mind. *There is no way to do life perfectly*, I echoed silently. Then: *There is no way to handle sexual assault perfectly. There is no way to lay your husband to rest perfectly. There is no way to move forward perfectly. PERFECT doesn't exist!*

And if perfect doesn't exist, the bar doesn't exist.

I don't have to jump over it, because it was never *actually there.*

Bells began clanging in my head. *Perfection is a perception. Perceptions change depending on who is doing the perceiving. Therefore, perfection is changeable and by definition cannot exist in a static, measurable form. Holy shit!*

You might think I felt relief in this moment. Eventually, I did. At first, though, all I felt was anger. *You mean I've wasted twenty-nine years chasing this fucking thing that was never even real?* I looked to my counselor and reported my revelation. "I have legitimately been reaching for this bar my whole life and I just now realized that that fucker never even existed. Do you know how much time and energy and effort and emotion I've wasted on trying to reach for something that was never even there? Unreal!"

The revelation didn't feel good—not right away—but as I drove away from her office I could feel the weight of perfection lifting off my shoulders. Brick by brick I felt lighter and free.

Every once in a while, a tidal wave of regret over the impossible standards I set for myself for so long comes pummeling to shore, and washes away the sandcastles I've been building in the sun. I then remember I'm on the shore, and done treading water. Safety, survival, self-love, and acceptance—these things are no longer out of reach, taunting me from a daunting distance. I—and you—have always done the best we could. While humanly flawed, our intentions were always good. And that makes us worthy.

CONCLUSION

ON FIGHT

Every year, I take Addisen to the beach in California. It's fun watching her grow up and into her own personality. Like I did when I was seven, she prefers to hang out on shore, playing in the sand and building mighty fortresses. I cheer her on, encouraging her to dream.

I never got the fairytale life I wanted: the white picket fence, the one forever husband, our multiple kids. And thank God for that! Because now, when Dodger and I sit in the beach chairs that my parents once occupied and ooh and aah over Addie's sandcastles, I am dually struck by the profundity of a life more beautiful than I ever imagined, and the amount of grit and fight it took to get it. The ebb and flow of the tide brings me peace, and staring at the ocean for hours, I find solace.

In the introduction to this book, I wrote that when you're floundering in life's storms, although standing on your own two feet again remains the goal, there are many ways to get back there. One of them—and the single most powerful in my own life to date—is to fight like hell to get there.

LETTING GO

Let's say you've chosen, in your life, to stay on shore, never to take any risks, because the threat of the undertow seems too great. What are you missing out on?

I would have missed out on *everything*. I might have tried, when I was younger, to see my life as perfect already, instead of chasing perfection. Then I would have been less impulsive in my decision-making: I never would have pulled into that recruiting station and joined the Navy. Without the Navy, I wouldn't have had Addisen. I wouldn't have met my soulmate, Sean. Wouldn't have made lifelong friends that today comprise my Circle of Trust. I might never have realized that "perfect" is a construct. I might still be waiting for my sandcastle life to manifest—might, in fact, be waiting forever.

If I'd stayed onshore, never tempted the riptide, I wouldn't have learned to tread. I would never have discovered, in near-death moments, that close calls are only that: an opportunity to dredge up forgotten reserves of strength, to practice perseverance, and save yourself. Then the next time something awful happened (as it will, because hurricanes come ashore, too) I wouldn't have the experience, the *evidence* to draw upon, to know that having survived before, I will again. Last but not least, I wouldn't have noticed the sun rise over the water. I would have taken it for granted, since I hadn't just spent the whole night fighting for the privilege.

Anyone can enjoy the beach when the water's calm and life is good. But what about the hardships, the monster waves that promise to sweep you away? Will you have the fight in you to withstand them? Will you trust yourself to do so? Will you have enough wisdom to know you can do both?

IDENTIFYING YOUR CIRCLE

Now when people come to me bent out of shape over the littlest of things that to them feel like giant problems, I recognize their problems for what they are: fixable. A problem is something we can work through and achieve a favorable outcome for. If the problem stems from inside that person, or is the result of a choice they made, I remind them that no matter how flawed they may feel, above all they're (still) worthy.

If you're not feeling worthy for whatever reason, you

need to find your Circle: those who love you and will dedicate their lives to proving your worth to you. Sometimes they're the ones who have been there from the beginning—in my case, Bridget. Occasionally, they come back into your life after a great absence, right when you need them most—like Dodger did for me. The rest of your Circle are the friends, colleagues, and mentors who stick it out through thick and thin, rough seas and calm ones, who don't disappear because you ran down a golf course screaming at a ghost from your past. You'll recognize them because they're the ones who are alongside you, cheering you on as you tread, never leaving your side even when they can't fight a particular battle with you. And they welcome you home, sopping and spent, after the long swim in.

Surrender to those people like you do a fight well-fought. Let them celebrate your successes *and* your shortcomings. Love them hard, with everything you've got, and never take the love they give you in return for granted.

BEAUTY IN THE PAIN

To all the young women out there in particular, treading water as single mothers or widows; who are working hard to better their lives, pursue educations, raise kids; who have been acutely or chronically sick, or are being abused, or are currently struggling with PTSD; God, I just want to reach through these pages and give you an encouraging embrace. I wish I could be your life preserver for a moment, so you can catch your breath, so you don't quit too soon. Just remember, you'll never know the blessings that are on the other side of giving up, if that's what you choose to do. In spite of the suffering, keep treading. There is beauty in the pain.

Pain is a teacher. Through pain, you learn gratitude. Through pain, you learn perseverance. Through pain, you learn to fight. Through pain, you learn to overcome. Pain doesn't give you the life you want, but the version you didn't know you needed.

Life never turned out the way I always dreamed it would, and as I reflect back on all the things I would've missed if it had, I thank God it never did. My current sandcastle and the family that resides inside of it look nothing like the fairytale I had planned out for myself all those years ago. If my younger self could be here to see it, she'd probably call it flawed. It'd be unworthy of her love. I'd then sit by her side, shoulder to shoulder, and whisper, *No, it's flawed, and* still *worthy of all your love.*

My mom Teresa, my dad Daryl, my older brother Luke, myself (at age 7), and Jessie our dog.

My parents Daryl and Teresa and my daughter Addisen.

Sean and me at the Navy Ball in 2011. Note Sean's dress blue uniform top. I wasn't able to let it go after his death.

Sean and me getting married at the courthouse!

Sean, me, and Addisen just before he died.

Receiving an American flag at Sean's funeral.

The flag gave me some comfort.

Sean's coffin.

My Circle of Trust at Dodger's and my wedding on November 17, 2017.

Dodger and I on our wedding day.

My sweet daughter Addisen.

Addisen again. I just love her!

Dodger, myself, and Addie.

ACKNOWLEDGMENTS

This book was born from the trials, tribulations, and tragedies of my life. It never would have come to fruition without the endless support of my family, friends, and mentors.

I have to start by thanking my incredible husband, Dodger. Your unwavering love through the ebbs and flows of this journey we call life has been awe-inspiring. You have never not championed a single dream of mine, including this one. Your encouragement and sacrifice throughout the entire writing process have been paramount to me finishing this book. I watched as you became super husband, keeping Addie entertained and stepping into roles I normally fill, so I could focus solely on this book. You have been my number one cheerleader over the course of this year and I can't thank you enough. I love you, babe!

I am eternally grateful for my late husband Sean, may he rest in peace. You were my beacon in the night, shining the light of your love into the darkest spaces of my soul. Your infectious laugh and contagious smile saw me through a plethora of setbacks and heartaches. You exemplified unconditional love, drawing out of me a certain amount of courage and strength I never knew I had. That love, strength, and courage stuck with me through your passing, allowing me to walk through the flames of pain that made it to the pages of this book. Your presence is sorely missed and your love lives on in the hearts you left behind. Thank you for everything, my love.

To my hardworking Daddy and Ma: You guys served as examples of how far hard work and grit can get you, and how love is the most important thing in the room. The solid foundation you built for me and the moral code you instilled in me have been the cornerstones that have led to any one of my successes. You have been a pillar to lean on, a shelter for solace, and a voice when I had none. As a direct result of your efforts, I had the grit and persistence to finish this book. I love you both, to the moon and back.

To my brother Luke: Thank you for the boogie-board-surfing, hooky-playing, dirt-jump-flying, advice-giving childhood and early adulthood we shared together. You were the best big brother and role model a little sister could ask for. I will never forget the bond we shared and the love we had for one another. Wherever life takes you, I know you will soar high. Love you, bubba.

Bridget Powers, somewhere along the way our kindergarten friendship morphed into an everlasting sisterhood. Through awkward stages of growing up to navigating adulthood, shoulder to shoulder, we have tackled it all. You have been and continue to be my biggest confidant and die-hard supporter, even when all the cards are stacked against me. Your fierce love and loyalty are unsurmountable. As a direct result of those two things, I was able to make it through the many hardships found within this book. I love you, Sissy. Thanks for being my number one.

It is my belief that every person on planet earth needs an Amy Abbott. Your no-bullshit, fully transparent, I'm-all-in attitude that you bring to our sisterhood is refreshing and incredibly rare. You have engulfed yourself in the flames of my pain more times than I can count, shouldering what you can, and talking me through what you can't. You are the type of friend who shows up every damn day without having to be asked. You hear words I do not say, fearlessly participate in battles that are not yours, and continuously state the truths everyone else is too scared to say. To my fire-breathing, water-treading, one-of-a-kind sister, thank you for showing me that pity is for pussies and fires are there to walk through, not around. Love you, Ames!

A big thank you to an old Master Chief whose famous phrase was to always "maintain my moral high ground": Shaun Peirsel. The death of Sean was unexpected, as was the lack of compassion and professionalism that directly followed. As a result, the responsibility of the transition from wife to widow inevitably landed on you. It was a role you never saw coming, but one you filled graciously. I was so angry at you—angry that you didn't tell me, angry that you couldn't protect me, angry that you couldn't protect Sean. Although my anger was unfair and misplaced, the sting from it never stopped you from showing up for me and fighting for Sean. With tear-stained cheeks and heavy eyes you paced outside of closed doors, yelled for answers through phones, and hopped on buses and planes for the sailor suffering in front of you and the sailor who went before you. Your unwavering support and perseverance during that time taught me the importance of answering the call and showing up, especially when it's unexpected. Most importantly, though, it taught me to always do the next best thing, even if it means doing it alone. Thank you for helping me navigate the hardest transition of my life. I will never forget all you did for me and the lessons you taught me in doing so.

To my aunt Deb, uncle Chad, and cousin Montana: Thank you for the love you've shown me over the years and the support you've given when it was needed most. I love you guys with all of my heart.

To Tara Gonga, David Valley, Hope Faivre, and Lisa Montgomery: Thank you for running to my aid on May 30, 2012. Bearing heavy hearts and open arms, you sat with me through awkward silences, loud cries of grief, and a million "I can't believe this is real life" screams. You were the life preservers that buoyed me up when I was unexpectedly launched into the volatile depths of a vast ocean. The love you showed me that day and all the days that followed will never be forgotten. I love you all.

John McConnell and Joseph Ring, thank you for bearing with me through the lows of my Naval career. Through the "What the fuck was she thinking" phone calls and the nail biting "I need to tell you something before it gets to you" statements, you never gave up on me. You showed me grace and forgiveness in place of anger and despair. You showed me a side of leadership that I hadn't experienced. I will never forget the kindness you both showed me through the darkest times of my life.

To Jess, Ellie, and the entire Lioncrest team: Thank you for your encouragement, support, and knowledge, as they have all made this book possible.

To all the friends, family, and strangers who have positively impacted my life: Whether it be for a moment or for years, thank you for blessing me with your light and love.

CPSIA information can be obtained
at www.ICGtesting.com
Printed in the USA
FSHW011249170320
68240FS